COWGIRLS COOK for the GREAT OUTDOORS

MORE THAN 90 HEARTY RECIPES for PICNICS, POTLUCKS, and PACK LUNCHES

JILL CHARLOTTE STANFORD
and Robin Betty Johnson

TWODOT®

GUILFORD, CONNECTICUT
HELENA, MONTANA

A · TWODOT® · BOOK

An imprint of Globe Pequot, the trade division of
The Rowman & Littlefield Publishing Group, Inc.
4501 Forbes Blvd., Ste. 200
Lanham, MD 2706
www.rowman.com

Distributed by NATIONAL BOOK NETWORK

British Library Cataloguing in Publication Information available

Library of Congress Cataloging-in-Publication Data

Names: Stanford, Jill Charlotte, author. | Johnson, Robin Betty, author.
Title: Cowgirls cook for the great outdoors : more than 90 delicious
recipes for picnics, potlucks, and pack lunches / Jill Charlotte
Stanford and Robin Betty Johnson.
Description: Guilford, Connecticut : TwoDot, [2022] | Includes
bibliographical references and index. | Summary: "More than ninety
recipes that the modern cowgirl needs to keep her crew fed and her
family happy on the trail or around the campfire. This cookbook combines
the best of cowgirl myths, nostalgia, and legends with useable,
delicious, and fun recipes for use in the great outdoors or at home"—
Provided by publisher.
Identifiers: LCCN 2021050440 (print) | LCCN 2021050441 (ebook) | ISBN
9781493048625 (paperback) | ISBN 9781493048632 (epub)
Subjects: LCSH: Cooking, American—Western style. | Outdoor cooking. |
LCGFT: Cookbooks.
Classification: LCC TX715.2.W47 S725 2022 (print) | LCC TX715.2.W47
(ebook) | DDC 641.5978—dc23/eng/20211028
LC record available at https://lccn.loc.gov/2021050440
LC ebook record available at https://lccn.loc.gov/2021050441

♾™ The paper used in this publication meets the minimum requirements of
American National Standard for Information Sciences—Permanence of Paper
for Printed Library Materials, ANSI/NISO Z39.48-1992

Dedicated to Karen Perkins

When a cowgirl dies and goes to Heaven, she does not get a halo. Instead, she gets a big, silver belt buckle.

—The Cowgirl's Cookbook: Recipes for Your Home on the Range

We knew a cowgirl who loved the outdoors and lived everything "Western." A fourth-generation Arizonian whose forebears drove their horses and cattle to the P6 ranch, now called Perkinsville, in 1900. Perkinsville is near Prescott. You get there by driving along a dusty, often snowy dirt road about ten or so miles. The Verde River flows through the property, and her favorite time of the year was autumn when the cottonwoods changed their color to a blaze of gold. She knew the West well, and she treasured the poetry, songs, music, and stories the old-timers would tell. Karen was a gifted artist. She drew and painted the ranch hands, cattle, and horses that she loved. She was a rodeo queen, a wife, a mother, a cook, a great ranch hand, and she was our friend.

Lorena Trickey was her favorite old-time cowgirl and she sent us many clippings and stories of this cowgirl she admired so much for her "grit and sand" as cowgirls are fond of saying about brave women.

Karen was brave to the very end—grit and sand. She rode that cancer almost to the whistle, never complaining. Her silver belt buckle in Heaven was waiting for her.

AUTHOR'S COLLECTION

CONTENTS

A NOTE FROM THE AUTHORS

When we were very little girls and the weather was fine, our mother would sometimes make a "picnic" for lunch, to be enjoyed on a blanket spread on the grass of our yard under a large maple tree. She would make peanut butter and honey sandwiches, which she assured us was what the baby bears had at "The Teddy Bears' Picnic." Or, she would make rose petal sandwiches—white bread, butter, fragrant Cecile Brunner rose petals from her garden, and sprinkled with sugar. Those, she said, were what the fairies enjoyed. With a glass of cold milk and perhaps a cookie, we remember those picnics with deep nostalgia.

We have always liked dining outdoors. A bonfire on the beach with hot dogs on a stick; a cook-out of coffee can stew on the shores of Puget

Very young cowgirls—Jill is six and Robin is almost one. They both grew up to be very good and innovative cooks. Credit: Author's Collection

Sound in the rain when we were Girl Scouts; a lobster feed on the shores of the Atlantic in Maine that will never be forgotten; a simple sandwich in our saddlebag; a friend's backyard barbecue with fireflies providing the evening's entertainment; a tailgate party for a football game in the rain; or the simple pieces of tender lamb skewered onto a juniper stick and cooked right in the flames of a campfire; breakfast around the campfire when horse camping with friends in the Deschutes National Forest. Catching, cleaning, and cooking a trout in an iron skillet balanced precariously over the coals is a lasting delight. (This was, of course, before "catch and release.")

Next to dining outdoors, gathering the harvest and bringing it home is a real pleasure with all that bounty of fruits and vegetables being made into jams, jellies, and pickles. Enjoying salads, fresh corn on the cob, or just eating the strawberries straight out of the container. In Vermont, we were delighted to find fresh fiddlehead ferns. Our friend goes mushrooming every fall and generously shares his wealth of chanterelle mushrooms, an edible woodland mushroom with a yellow, funnel-shaped cap and a faint smell of apricots. We loved picking blackberries right off the vine (never mind the thorns!) in the late summer sun, knowing there would be a pie later that evening, as well as jam to be spread on toast on cold and snowy winter mornings.

The outdoors offers us so much. Besides food to harvest or catch or pick and prepare, it offers a simpler way of life, and a slower one. We hear the wind, we listen to the birds or the stream, we gaze out over the lake from the saddle or the folding chairs in front of our camper or tent. Perhaps we are just out on our porch or sitting in front of an open window in the sun. As long as there is fresh air, and you are out in it, what you eat out there is—to our way of thinking—a picnic.

It is with pleasure that we offer to you the recipes, tips, and ideas we've rounded up to help you get outside into the great outdoors and to enjoy all the bounty Mother Nature has so thoughtfully provided.

—Jill Charlotte Stanford   —Robin Betty Johnson
Sisters, Oregon   Portland, Oregon

ACKNOWLEDGMENTS

A tip of our straw hats to the following for their willingness to share and help in so many ways:

Jim Johnson, Robin's husband, who built campfires, fixed my camera, carried everything, sampled everything we came up with, and made suggestions. He was always honest about it, too.

Cindy Forbes of Ronan, Montana. It was my very great pleasure to meet Cindy on a beautiful late summer day. She shared a recipe with us that to this day we can't seem to get right.

Lorrie Turner who shared stories of her mother and recipes perfect for the ride you take or the table you set.

Jan Shipman who, literally, saddled right up and sent me a photo of her and her trail partner, Bull, plus the recipe for her trail mix she takes on her rides.

Coi Drummond-Gehring, Denver Museum, who has been my "go-to" person for historic photographs for quite a few of my books.

Harney County Historical Society was helpful and their quick response was so appreciated!

Montana History Project provided us with quite a few lovely old photos of gardens and picnics "back in the old days."

Lauralee Northcott provided valuable, and often funny, advice on horse camping as well as a wonderful poem she wrote.

Janice Gilbertson, who is no stranger to horse camping, shared a recipe and a dandy picture, too.

Gail James, from England, who visited the Great Basin of Washington State and became a real cowgirl. She shared what the Brits take on a picnic.

Rod Castelda was very shy about asking if we would be interested in the foolproof, indestructible sandwich he made as a boy picking peaches in the Yakima Valley of Washington State.

Special thanks to Chef Instructor Clive Wanstall, CCE, who teaches at Lane Community College in Eugene for his tips and hints for food safety in the great outdoors.

And last but not least, not by a long shot, my editor, Erin Turner. She started us down this trail. She handed the reins to Sarah Parke who brought the whole thing, strays and all, to the book you have in your hands.

INTRODUCTION: BEFORE YOU GO—ADVICE FROM A COWGIRL

Winston Churchill said, "There is nothing better for the inside of a man than the outside of a horse," and we agree wholeheartedly. However, we'd like to change this just a little bit: "There is nothing better for the inside of a *cowgirl* than the outside."

Whether you are going on a simple one- or two-hour trail ride, a packing-in horse camp trip of several days, a road trip to a scenic spot in your RV, or a hike into the woods, it makes no difference in the preparations you should make before stepping out the door into "the great outdoors." A picnic is *always* a good idea, and it can be simple or elaborate because the choices are up to you.

Perhaps, as you are driving to or returning from an adventure in the outdoors, you pass a roadside produce stand? By all means, STOP, because a bounty of goodness is there that you can take home or to your campsite and prepare immediately, or preserve for gray and dreary days when you can't get outdoors.

Whatever your choice of getting outdoors for an hour, a day, or longer, there are certain precautions to take and things to have on hand. You are, after all, a long way from the supermarket.

We asked a "professional" cowgirl who has been Out There and

Lauralee Northcott
Credit: Courtesy of Lauralee Northcott

came back to tell us what we ought to remember to take and (more importantly *not* take) on our adventures. Heed her words. Make a list, check it twice, tighten your cinches, fill up your gas tank, and GO.

We'd like to introduce you to a cowgirl who knows her way around a mountain, often on a barely discernible trail, leading a packhorse or two with a line of happy campers strung out on horseback behind her. Lauralee Northcott has spent her summers as a guide and cook for groups camping and traveling in the North Cascades. At the end of the trail, the campers will be fed delicious foods, cooked over the campfire by Lauralee, and, following their meal, Lauralee will recite some of her poetry (we've included one of her poems) and end the evening with a song she has written. This is valuable advice from Lauralee for your foray into the wilderness and quite a bit of it holds true for backpacks, RVs, and tent camping, as well.

"Each type of adventure requires a unique set of items but luckily, I am a list person and I encourage you to be one too. I am happy to share with you a few lists honed from years of experience in the great outdoors. I'll share saddlebag contents, my clothing, and the camp kitchen items."

On the Trail: Your Saddlebags Checklist

A word about saddlebags. Leather or canvas saddlebags are both fine as long as they are rainproof. The main thing is to keep the contents of the saddlebags light. No more than three pounds to a side because the saddlebags sit right over the horse's kidneys. A rider moves with the horse, but the saddlebags are dead weight slapping up and down. This can affect your horse's long-term health.

- Your lunch or trail snack, wrapped well and keeping cold with a small cold pack

- Sunblock

- Bug repellant

- Water bottle

- Matches (in a zip-top bag)

- Fire starter (a piece or two of pitch wood)

- Leatherman—a super useful knife, usually worn on the belt, but if not, then in your saddlebags

- Wire, duct tape, and cord (quick repairs are sometimes needed)

- First aid kit

- Flashlight with fresh batteries

- Leather gloves

- Toilet paper or handy-wipes (both eco-friendly)

- Maps of the area and a compass

- Benadryl/Ibuprofen

- Hoof pick

- Foil blanket (emergency supply, quite small)

Camping Gear

Camping is a great way to get outside into the great outdoors with your horse, friends, or by yourself. You can go camping in many state and national parks, at private campgrounds, and in the backcountry. Many states have horse camps that include a picnic table, a place to park your truck and trailer, small individual corrals, and a spot to pitch your tent or throw down your sleeping bag to sleep under the stars. Many also have shared bathrooms and running water. The biggest bonus of a horse camp, in my eyes, is that you can pack everything into your truck as well as your trailer (besides the horse, of course). No need for a pack horse.

You need very little gear to camp outdoors, but it's also nice to have a comfortable and convenient campsite. If it's your first time camping, it might be best to borrow some of these things. It can get a little pricey and what if you don't enjoy it? Personally, we can't see that happening at all! As you become a more experienced camper, you may find that part of the fun is figuring out what to bring along to meet your needs because you might have, like me, learned the hard way and brought Too Much Stuff the First Time.

If you are simply going on an overnight campout, your needs are simple. Two or three days and it gets a little more complicated. But with a list, you can do it. *Just think it out, hour by hour and day by day.* Pick and choose depending on where you are going and how long. Or, go to a reputable sporting goods store and have a look around. The people who work there usually have done exactly what you are planning on doing and can offer helpful hints and tips.

You can find complete lists of camping gear online, but we'll list the food-related essentials here:

- A large plastic tote for all your carefully thought-out food, along with cold packs or ice and zip-top bags

- A cast iron skillet for dinner and breakfast

- An old coffee pot

- Coffee, measured for your coffee pot, in a zip-top lock bag

- Cooking utensils, like a spatula, slotted spoon, forks, and knives

HORSE CAMPING

Many people have asked us how to find horse camps all over the United States. It could not be easier. Just Google "horse camps" and the state you're looking for, and it's all there at your fingertips.

Most of them require reservations. You can also stop in at any state park office for free maps of where you will be riding or hiking. Always have a map handy. Google Maps is a good source of highway distances for places to RV camp as well.

Now get out there into the great outdoors!

- Stainless steel plates and/or bowls

- Stainless steel mugs

- Salt and pepper (and other spices) in small zip-top bags

- Sugar for your coffee or tea in a small zip-top bag

- Trash bags to carry everything out

Now, wasn't that easy? You can do it! We know you can. So off you go. Have a wonderful time.

Chapter 1
BREAKFASTS TO JUMP-START YOUR DAY

Beer Batter Pancakes with Citrus Bourbon Syrup

MAKES 8 PANCAKES

Cowgirl Lorrie Turner told us, "Growing up in southern Idaho on a farm we learned from our dad that milk is not always necessary. He made these pancakes when he would go hunting with the guys, but one Saturday night we wanted pancakes for dinner but were out of milk! So Dad made these for us, against my mother's wishes I might add, and they quickly became our favorite!"

1¼ cup sifted all-purpose flour
¼ cup sugar
¾ teaspoon baking powder
½ teaspoon salt
¼ teaspoon cinnamon
1 egg
1 cup light beer
2 tablespoons butter, melted
½ teaspoon vanilla extract

In a small bowl stir together all dry ingredients. In a separate bowl stir together wet ingredients. Add the dry ingredients to the wet ingredients stirring just until combined. (It's OK if the batter is a little lumpy.)

Cook on a hot griddle until bubbles form and pop, then turn and cook on the other side until browned, about 3 to 5 minutes on each side.

CITRUS BOURBON SYRUP

1 cup sugar
1 cup light brown sugar
½ cup water
½ cup orange juice
Zest of 1 navel orange
1 cup bourbon of choice (the cowgirls' preference is, of course, Pendleton Whisky!)

In a saucepan combine the sugars, water, orange juice, and orange zest.

Bring to a boil and then simmer on low until mixture is reduced by half and slightly thick.

Remove from the heat and stir in the bourbon.

Campfire Coffee

ONE POT—YOUR CHOICE OF SIZE

The Cowgirl's Cookbook featured this coffee made over a campfire in a battered coffee pot. Our trail friend Joie Smith taught this to us. Joie was an accomplished outdoorswoman, knowledgeable in all aspects of camping. A never-to-be-forgotten remark was made by her, casually, over her shoulder to the riders behind her on the trail: "You'll want to stay alert. That's fresh bear scat." Believe me when we say we were alert for hours after that. She has ridden ahead to that great camp out in the sky, but whenever we have this coffee, we think of her. You will need an old coffee pot, the kind that "perks."

2 heaping tablespoons ground coffee per person

1 tablespoon salt

1 cup fresh, cold water per person

1 eggshell, broken into medium-size pieces

Pour the water into the pot. Add the coffee and the salt.

Place the pot over the hot coals, on a grill, or suspended by a pole over the fire.

When the coffee starts to perk or boil, remove the pot from the fire and put in the eggshells. The shells cause the coffee grounds to settle to the bottom of the pot.

Keep the coffee warm beside the fire, but do not allow it to boil again.

Bury the grounds under a tree when you are cleaning up.

COWBOY COFFEE

From *A Cowgirl's Life in the Mountains* by Lauralee Northcott

I love the smell of coffee,
In the cook tent at early dawn.
Just like a big old welcome to the day,
it puts a stopper in my yawn.

Cowboy coffee,
Is just a delicious drink.
It's warm, it's cheap, and it wakes you up.
But it's harder to make than you'd think.

I've seen so many try it,
And make a boiled-over mess.
Or else that flavorless, tea-ish stuff,
that looks like, you can guess.

So here's a tip for the novice cook,
Get that water boiling hard.
Then put in a big old scoop of grounds,
And watch it buck, old pard.

It's gotta boil and then turns over,
Sorta like a milfoil in a pond,
And when it gets that saddle-brown,
You've got the flavor of which we're fond.

Put in a little cold water,
That makes the grounds sink
Then you've got a cup of Joe
That everyone will love to drink.

I'm just an old camp cook,
And I'm not very hip,
But if you can make a good pot of cowboy coffee,
You just might get a tip!

Campout Bread

SERVES 8

Here is a great thing to cook over the coals or in your home oven in your new—or old—8-inch cast iron skillet with a lid or a piece of aluminum foil to fit the top. If you are headed into the great outdoors, read this recipe carefully before you leave, and be sure you have all the ingredients bagged and ready. Or, get out your mixing bowls at home and preheat the oven to 350°F.

4 tablespoons dried buttermilk
¼ teaspoon salt
1 tablespoon baking powder
¼ ounce fast-acting dry yeast
½ teaspoon cardamom
¾ teaspoon cinnamon
3 tablespoons sugar
1½ cups all-purpose flour
½ cup raisins
½ cup chopped walnuts (optional)
1 cup warm (100–110°F) water
1 tablespoon shortening

In a mixing bowl, combine the dry ingredients: buttermilk, salt, baking powder, yeast, cardamom, cinnamon, sugar, flour, raisins, and the optional nuts. Mix together well. (**Note:** If you are taking this for camping, put the dry mixture in a zip-top bag.)

When ready to bake, add the warm water into the dry ingredients and blend well, until it resembles a thick cake batter.

Coat the bottom and the sides of the 8-inch cast iron skillet well with the shortening. Pour the batter into the skillet, cover with the lid or the piece of aluminum foil, and let the dough rise in a draft-free, warm place for about 20 to 25 minutes.

Take off the lid or aluminum foil (save for cleanup) and cook over low embers of a campfire (raise the grill from the embers) or low on a camp stove for 25 to 30 minutes. You can also bake it on the lowest rack in your oven for about 25 minutes. The usual "poking with a clean, thin stick" method will tell you if it is baked clear through.

Country Girls' Gravy and Biscuits

SERVES 4

We don't know who said "You can take the girl out of the country, but you can't take the country out of the girl," but we know it's true, especially when it comes to food! Let's face it—the best things are the simple things, like this classic for breakfast, lunch, or dinner, indoors or out. If you have a stovetop in your RV and it's pouring rain outside, make this. Or mix it all up in the cast iron skillet.

1 pound lean ground beef

½ white onion, finely chopped

3 tablespoons all-purpose flour

1½–2 cups whole milk

2 tablespoons Worcestershire sauce (Robin likes A-1 Steak Sauce)

Salt and pepper, to taste

4 biscuits in a zip-top bag (we used Pillsbury Grands!™)

Heat a cast iron skillet and crumble the beef into it. Fry it on medium-high, stirring to break up any lumps.

Add the onions to the pan, stirring until they are translucent and the beef is cooked through.

Sprinkle the flour over the beef and onions and stir until a thick paste is made. Then *slowly* pour the milk into the pan, stirring constantly, and—presto—you have gravy.

Bring to a boil, stirring, until the gravy has thickened. Turn the heat down and add the steak sauce and salt and pepper.

Serve over a split biscuit or a thick slice of toast.

COWGIRL DAREDEVIL BONNIE McCARROLL

Bonnie McCarroll was born Mary Ellen Treadwell in 1897 on a cattle ranch at High Valley, near Boise, Idaho. She was nicknamed "Dot." Bonnie was known as a daredevil early on, riding rank horses. She went on to ride the rodeos, and in her first year of competition in 1915, she won two cowgirl bronc riding championships at both the Cheyenne, Wyoming, Frontier Days and the first rodeo hosted at Madison Square Garden in New York City. There was nothing Bonnie didn't try or excel at, including steer riding (you read that right!), bulldogging, and even jumping over automobiles, often with passengers ducking inside!

Over the course of her career, she performed before kings, queens, and President Calvin Coolidge. The Pendleton Round-Up of September 1929 was to have been McCarroll's final competition. She had planned to retire with her husband, Frank Leo McCarroll, to their home in Boise. While giving a bronc riding exhibition, Bonnie met an unfortunate end when she was thrown from a bucking horse named Black Cat. We think she might have liked it that way.

This image of her is handprinted on a tin coffee can and was sent to me by an admirer of my Cowgirl books.

Credit: Author's Collection

Cowgirls' Breakfast Skillet

SERVES 8

Breakfast in the great outdoors should be a great hearty meal to get your day going. There is a very fancy word for this egg dish—"frittata," which is Spanish for omelette. We simply call it "good"! The beauty of this recipe is you can add or subtract as you wish to make it your own.

2 tablespoons olive oil

6 eggs

3 tablespoons milk (full-fat highly recommended)

1 cup shredded or crumbled cheese of your choice (we recommend cheddar), plus a little more for sprinkling on top

½ teaspoon salt

½ teaspoon pepper

1 cup diced sweet onion

½ cup chopped red pepper, seeded and cut into 2-inch-long lengths

½ cup chopped yellow pepper, seeded and cut into 2-inch-long lengths

1 (4-ounce) can green chiles, drained, seeded, and cut into smaller pieces

Preheat the oven to 350°F.

Heat olive oil in a 10-inch skillet over a low flame.

In a medium bowl, stir eggs with a fork until the egg yolks and whites are just barely blended. Add the milk, cheese, salt, and pepper, and stir well. Set aside.

Into the heated skillet, add the onion, peppers, and green chiles. Stir and cook these vegetables until nearly done, then pour the egg mixture into the skillet. Add more cheese over the top, and let it cook, still on low, for about 8 to 10 minutes. Watch for the edges to turn a lighter color.

Pop it in the oven and bake for about 10 minutes. It will puff up and the middle should be a little bit "loose"—not set.

Take it out of the oven to cool before cutting like a pie. This dish is wonderful served with sour cream and also tasty as a cold left-over for lunch when you return from the first ride.

Here are a few variations to try:

- Spinach, sliced black olives, artichoke bottoms, and feta cheese in and on top
- Broccoli florets, shredded cheddar, and chopped green onion with shredded cheddar melted on top
- Mushrooms, two kinds of onion (sweet white and green), with mozzarella on top
- Cherry tomatoes, chopped mozzarella, and basil with shredded mozzarella on top
- Diced ham into any of the above
- And it just goes on and on . . . what will you add to make it your very own?

Cowgirls' Easy Chicken and Waffles

SERVES 5-6

Here is a great dish to serve up for breakfast, lunch, or dinner in your RV. You'll need an icebox or electric cooler and at least one burner and an oven (or microwave) to create the simplest, most delicious combo ever invented in our opinion. You can thank the Amish for this version, although we are fairly certain they raised and cooked the chicken, and so forth. This recipe takes shortcuts with frozen waffles and a pre-made jar of chicken gravy.

1 (12-ounce) jar chicken gravy
1 rotisserie chicken, boned, skinned, and cut or torn into bite-size pieces
1 box frozen waffles (10–12 waffles)

Preheat the oven to 350°F.

Warm the jar of chicken gravy in a saucepan. Or, you make your own gravy (recipe follows).

Add the chicken pieces into the gravy to heat through, remembering to stir it.

Place the waffles on a cookie sheet and heat on the lowest oven rack for 5 to 8 minutes, turning them halfway through the heating. (**Cowgirl tip:** If you don't have an oven, wrap the waffles in foil on the grill.)

Put two hot waffles on each plate, then spoon the chicken and gravy over them. Didn't we say this was going to be easy?

Does it get any better than this?

Well, real purists pour a little maple syrup over all this, too, and we think that is a fine idea!

And the Amish add an ice cream scoop of mashed potatoes on the side.

HOMEMADE CHICKEN GRAVY
ABOUT 3 CUPS

If you prefer to make your own chicken gravy before you travel, here's a simple and delicious recipe.

½ stick (4 tablespoons) butter
¼ cup all-purpose flour
2 cups chicken stock or broth
¼ cup half-and-half or whole milk
Salt and pepper, to taste

Melt the butter in a saucepan over medium heat, then sprinkle the flour evenly over the melted butter and whisk together.

Next add the chicken stock. The flour mixture will clump up, but hang in there and continue to cook, stirring or whisking frequently, until the clumps are gone and the gravy has turned a lovely golden color. It will remain pale for a few minutes, then toast quickly, so keep an eye on it.

Add the half-and-half and cook, stirring all the time, until the gravy thickens and comes to a simmer.

Remove from the heat and season with salt and pepper to taste. Add in the chicken.

Keep this cool in an airtight container or the icebox until ready to serve.

Early Riser Seasonal Fruit Salad with Granola, Yogurt, and Ruby Rhubarb Sauce

SERVES 2

Granola with fruit is a perfect, healthy alternative to any camping breakfast, particularly if you put it on top of your favorite yogurt and then top it with one of these seasonal fruit renditions.

2 cups of your preferred granola
1–2 cups plain or flavored yogurt (it's all about your tastes)
Seasonal fruit (see suggestions below)
Ruby Rhubarb Sauce (for topping)

In a bowl or your favorite camping mug, layer granola and yogurt with your choice of seasonal fruit combinations (see suggestions below). Top with a generous pour of Ruby Rhubarb Sauce (see below).

RUBY RHUBARB SAUCE
MAKES 1½ CUPS

3 cups fresh rhubarb, cut into ½-inch pieces
1 cup sugar
1 tablespoon lemon juice
1 tablespoon water

Combine the cut rhubarb, sugar, lemon juice, and water in a medium saucepan. Cook over medium heat, stirring frequently until the rhubarb softens, about 6 to 8 minutes. Taste and add additional lemon juice or sugar and water until it is a taste and consistency that you like. Finished sauce should be fairly thick.

Store in the refrigerator; this also freezes well.

Other seasonal options:

- Spring Salad: 1 cup strawberries tossed with ½ cup Ruby Rhubarb Sauce

- Summer Salad: 1 cup fresh peaches and plums, cut up, tossed with ½ cup raspberries and blueberries

- Fall Salad: 1 cup pears and apples, peeled and chopped, tossed with a ¼ cup cranberry sauce, and a pinch of cinnamon

- Winter Salad: 1 cup mixed grapefruit, oranges, pineapple, and bananas, tossed with 1 tablespoon honey

Note: You can take any one of these selections and make a healthy "banana split" by splitting a banana and using yogurt along with the sauce as your topping.

Good Morning Breakfast Burritos

SERVES 4

For this recipe, we recommend prepping many of the ingredients (bacon, green onions, peppers, rice) before you go on your great outdoor adventure, so you are ready to warm the tortillas and scramble the eggs and assemble.

4 large flour tortillas

6–8 strips bacon, cut in ½-inch pieces

8 green onions, chopped

½ large sweet red pepper, cut into
  ¼-inch strips

1 cup cooked brown rice (½ cup
  uncooked makes 1 cup)

½ cup black beans warmed (optional)

6 large eggs

1 tablespoon milk or cream

3 tablespoons butter

Toppings:

Salsa (We hope you will use ours,
  Cowgirl Crude Salsa, found on
  page 77.)

Grated cheddar cheese

Sour cream

Cilantro

Wrap the tortillas in foil and warm over the fire or in a 300°F oven.

Fry the bacon until crisp and set aside.

Chop the green onions and set aside.

Slice the red pepper and set aside.

Bring 1 cup of water to a boil in a small saucepan and then add the rice. Cover and cook at a simmer for 20 to 30 minutes until the rice is tender.

Crack the eggs into a large bowl and add 1 tablespoon milk. Using a whisk, whisk the eggs until they are very frothy and well combined, about a minute.

Heat a cast iron skillet at medium-low, melt the butter, and add the eggs. They will start to cook slowly, and using a spatula, gently cook and move the eggs around until they are done to your liking.

Each camper can assemble a warm tortilla by adding scrambled eggs, bacon, onions, peppers, and rice, and then add your choice of the garnishes (salsa, cheese, sour cream, and cilantro).

Hash It Up

This is a good one-pan hash for breakfast served with eggs over easy. Feel free to add or subtract ingredients depending on your likes or what you have handy at the campsite.

1 cup chorizo (or any other breakfast sausage)

2 tablespoons butter

3 cups red potatoes, cut into ½-inch pieces with skins on

1 cup chopped red onion

1 cup cooked corn, cut off the cob (or canned is fine)

1 cup cherry tomatoes, cut in half

½ cup shredded cheddar cheese

2 eggs per person

Sour cream (optional)

Ketchup (optional)

Fry the sausage in a cast iron skillet or Dutch oven until it is well-cooked, about 10 minutes. Remove from the pan and set aside.

Add 1 tablespoon of butter to the pan, let it melt, and then add the cut up red potatoes on medium-high heat to start the browning process.

Continue to cook on medium-high for about 5 minutes, stirring quite often.

Turn the heat down to medium-low or move the pan away from the heat, and continue to cook the potatoes for another 10 to 15 minutes, stirring often, until they are crispy on the outside and soft in the middle. Remove them from the pan and set aside.

Add another tablespoon of butter to the pan and add the red onions. Cook them for about 5 minutes on medium-low heat. To this onion mix, add back in the sausage and potatoes, and stir. Now add the corn and cherry tomatoes and let this all warm through.

Sprinkle with the cheese.

Fry your eggs and serve on the hash with the optional sour cream (Robin's choice) and/or ketchup (Jill's choice).

Oatmeal Pancakes with Blueberries and Crisp Bacon

MAKES 8 PANCAKES

What could be better than bacon and pancakes served up on a crisp and sunny morning before a day of hiking, trail riding, or yawning your way out of your RV to greet the dawn? These pancakes have the added ingredient of oatmeal that will "stick to your ribs" and help keep you going until lunch.

1 pound bacon

For the pancakes:

1 cup all-purpose flour
½ cup instant oatmeal
1½ tablespoon sugar
1½ teaspoon baking powder
¾ teaspoon baking soda
¾ teaspoon salt
½ teaspoon cinnamon (optional)
2 eggs
1 cup yogurt
1 cup milk (may need more to thin out pancake batter if it's not used right away)
3 tablespoons butter, melted
1 cup blueberries

Fry bacon in a cast iron skillet over the fire, camp stove, or RV stove until crispy and then drain on paper towels. Who doesn't love the smell of bacon in the woods? Reserve 2 tablespoons bacon drippings to further season the cast iron pan for the pancakes.

Combine dry ingredients (flour through cinnamon) in a bowl and whisk them together well. (We recommend pre-measuring and combining the dry ingredients in a zip-top bag before heading out.)

Combine wet ingredients in a larger bowl and mix well. Add the dry ingredients to the wet ingredients and mix gently until just combined. (**Note:** Instant oatmeal is thirsty and if you don't use your batter right away it will drink the wet ingredients making for a thick batter. Thin it down with more milk if necessary.)

Heat the cast iron skillet on medium heat and brush with the reserved bacon drippings. Make smaller pancakes (2 to 3 inches across) turning them only once in the cooking process.

Serve with the crispy bacon, butter, and warm syrup. Add ripe blueberries on top of your pancakes and enjoy the morning!

Sun's-Up Cornmeal and Banana Tacos

SERVES 2

Cowgirl Robin came up with this and Jill thinks it is brilliant. An unusually delicious way to start the day! We'd serve this with a side of fresh fruit and some really strong coffee.

¼ cup almonds (or any nut of your choice), toasted and chopped
4 small (6-inch) cornmeal tortillas
3 ripe bananas
½ stick (4 tablespoons) butter
½ cup brown sugar
1 teaspoon vanilla
½ teaspoon cinnamon
1 teaspoon lemon juice
1 cup plain Greek yogurt
3 tablespoons honey

Preheat the oven to 350°F.

Toast nuts for 5 to 6 minutes until fragrant. Let cool, then chop and set aside. (Camping alternative: Pan roast the nuts at medium heat in a cast iron skillet over a camp stove for the same amount of time. This is a good item to bring already prepped and ready to use.)

Wrap the tortillas in foil and warm them in an oven at 350°F or at the side of a BBQ grill or campfire until ready to serve.

Peel and cut the bananas in half and then again lengthwise (trying to match the width of your 6-inch tortillas for wrapping).

Melt the butter in a cast iron skillet on the stove or camp stove or grated fire pit. Add the brown sugar, vanilla, cinnamon, and lemon juice. Bring it to a simmer and cook 1 or 2 minutes until smooth and glossy and the sugar is dissolved.

Add the bananas and almonds to the pan and cook gently for another 3 or 4 minutes and set aside.

Combine the yogurt and honey and set aside.

Assemble the tacos by laying out the warm tortillas. Spread 3 or 4 tablespoons of honey yogurt on each tortilla, arrange several bananas on top, and fold to make a taco. Repeat until you have used all the tortillas.

To keep these warm place them on a baking sheet, cover with foil, and place back in a 300°F oven or in the cast iron covered with foil over the fire until ready to serve.

Sunrise Scones

MAKES 6 SCONES

Let us introduce you to the Omnia Oven*. It is the ideal solution for baking on propane burner camp stoves, gas, electric, kerosene, and even on a grill. It's also known as a wonder pot and no wonder! You can bake brownies, cakes, breads, casseroles, and more on any stovetop. Robin is an avid devotee of this oven and she shares a scone recipe for you to try in it on your next camping trip.

2½ cups all-purpose flour
1 tablespoon sugar
2 teaspoons baking powder
½ teaspoon salt
⅓ cup shortening or softened butter
½ cup milk or half-and-half

Heat the Omnia Oven on high for a few minutes and then turn down to 250°F. (There are complete instructions that come with this little miracle machine.)

Whisk the flour, sugar, baking powder, and salt together in a large bowl. (**Cowgirl tip:** Prepare all this before you go, and put the ingredients in a zip-top bag.)

Cut the shortening or butter into the dry mixture with a fork until it's a crumbly texture.

Add the milk all at once and mix gently until just combined. Don't overmix, please.

Turn the dough out on a floured board and knead briefly until it just comes together.

Pat the dough into two equal circles, each about ¾-inch thick. Cut the circles into four equal quarters and place on a baking sheet lined with parchment paper.

Place half the scones on the rack in the Omnia Oven.

Bake for 15 minutes—they will brown some but, full disclosure, not as well as a conventional oven.

Bake the second batch while you enjoy the first with butter and jam, or butter and honey!

*See Sources in the back of this book for more information and where to find it.

Chapter 2

SNACKS FOR YOUR SADDLEBAG OR BACKPACK

CENTRAL OREGON COWGIRLS

The day and the outdoors await for whatever adventure lies ahead. This wonderful image of two girls on their horses herding cattle are the Johnson sisters, Emma (Johnson) Krumbein and Ella (Johnson) Dillon. Here are Emma and Ellen herding their family's cattle on their ranch at Lawen, which was seventeen miles east of Burns, Oregon, around 1908. It's interesting to note that they are dressed as "ladies" in riding skirts, hats, and boots. You have to wonder if the person who took their picture also brought them lunch? And what was that lunch?

Credit: Claire McGill Luce Western History Room, Harney County LibraryT2

Berry Good Oatmeal Bars

MAKES 6 LARGE BARS

We can tell you on good authority that baked goods are absolutely wonderful in Sweden. Robin was visiting Sweden and discovered these tasty oatmeal bars made with lingonberry, a berry found there. She decided to re-create them and we think she did a darn good job! These are good no matter what fruit preserve or jam you try.

½ cup old-fashioned oats
1¼ cups all-purpose flour
¾ cup dark brown sugar
1 teaspoon baking powder
¾ teaspoon cinnamon
½ teaspoon cardamom
½ cup almonds, finely chopped
1½ sticks (12 tablespoons) salted
    butter, cut into small pieces
2 teaspoons vanilla extract
1–1¼ cups fruit jam or jelly

Preheat the oven to 350°F.

Lightly grease an 8 x 8-inch or 11 x 7-inch baking pan. Then line the pan with parchment to cover the bottom and come up and over the sides of the pan to make a sling for easy lifting out when the bars are done.

Combine the oats, flour, brown sugar, baking powder, and spices in a medium bowl and whisk well.

Add the butter and work this into the dry mixture with a fork—or your hands will do just fine—until combined and crumbly. Add the vanilla and mix again.

Put two-thirds of the mixture in the parchment-lined pan and press lightly to pat down the mixture. Spread about 1 to 1¼ cups of your choice of jam or jelly evenly over the pressed-in dough.

Sprinkle the remaining dough in the pan and again gently pat it down.

Bake for 30 minutes. Let cool completely. Using the sling created by the parchment, lift the bars out and cut them as you please.

Options: As we mentioned above, you can make these using any berry jam or preserves. Leave out the cardamom and you then have a fruit oatmeal bar. Get creative—use Apple Pumpkin Butter (see recipe on page 135) and sprinkle raisins on the fruit for a fall bar. Use peach or blackberry jam and no spices and add a little lemon zest over the jam for a summer bar. Great trail food!

Cheese and Chive Bites

MAKES 3 DOZEN BISCUITS

You've been out all day sightseeing, hiking, fishing, and so on, and when you get back to your "home away from home" it's nice to have an adult beverage. What to have with that welcome drink while the grill is heating up or the campfire is getting ready? These cheesy biscuits! They are easy to make, require few ingredients, and best of all, they freeze well so you can make a batch or two, put as many as you like in a zip-top bag, and you are ready to roll. Pairs well with a nice red wine.

1 stick (½ cup) butter, softened
2 tablespoons cream cheese, softened (not the whipped kind, please)
2 cups grated cheddar cheese
1½ cups all-purpose flour
½ teaspoon salt
1 tablespoon dried chives
½ teaspoon cayenne pepper or dried red pepper flakes (optional)

Preheat your oven to 350°F.

In a medium-size bowl, combine the butter, cream cheese, and cheddar cheese.

Now add the flour, salt, and chives. If you want to add a "kick," sprinkle ½ teaspoon of cayenne pepper or ½ teaspoon of dried red pepper flakes to the dough.

Mix this until you know you have a good, well-blended dough.

Take a pinch of the dough and roll it between your (clean) hands to form a ¾- to 1-inch ball.

Place the dough ball on an ungreased cookie sheet (or a cookie sheet lined with parchment paper). Use the tines of a fork to flatten the ball to a round disk about ¼ inch thick.

Now prick the round with the fork tines several times.

Repeat these steps until you have filled your cookie sheet(s).

Bake for 12 to 18 minutes. The biscuits should be very lightly browned around the edges.

Remove them to a wire rack to cool completely.

To freeze, put the cooled biscuits back on the cookie sheet and freeze them until solid. Then transfer them to a zip-top bag. You can reheat these in the oven.

Cowgirl Jill's Beef Jerky

MAKES 12-14 SLICES OF JERKY

"Jerk" has been around for a long, long time. Dried meat provided a portable form of nourishment for the travelers of the plains. Any meat will do, but beef is, in my opinion, the perfect snack to take on your trail ride. It is surprisingly easy to make, if a little time-consuming, but once you make it, you will make it again. It travels well in a plastic bag, takes up very little room in your saddlebags, and will give you a boost. Truly worth the effort.

1 pound beef—flank steak is best to use
Liquid smoke
Water
Salt

Trim the meat well, removing all the fat. Cut the meat into thin strips 4 to 8 inches in length.

In a 9 x 9-inch glass dish, make a mixture of two parts liquid smoke to one part water.

Dip each strip of meat into this mixture and then lay it flat in another glass dish.

When you have one layer of dipped meat in the dish, sprinkle it liberally with table salt.

Repeat until the dish is about three-quarters full. This process gets very "juicy" and the dish will overflow if it is too full. If you have more meat, use another dish.

Cover the dish (or dishes) with plastic wrap and put them in a cool place for 24 hours.

Preheat your oven to 140°F or the lowest setting.

Put a flat pan with aluminum foil on the very bottom of the oven to catch the drips. Lay the strips (unrinsed) across the oven racks, using as many racks as you can.

Bake for 10 to 12 hours until the meat is free of moisture but not brittle.

Store in glass jars or put the strips into sandwich-size zip-top bags in the freezer to grab as you head out the door.

Honey of a Snack Bar

MAKES 6 MEDIUM BARS OR 12 BITE-SIZE PIECES

This is a sweet, crunchy, chewy snack to take on a hike or a trail ride or to the movies. Thanks to Jean Winthrop for this recipe—she sent me a bag of it and we begged for more. This cowgirl spends her time on horseback, riding her fence lines in Nebraska. A snack is always welcome.

6 tablespoons butter
1/3 cup firmly packed brown sugar
1/4 cup honey
3 cups any good granola you like

Preheat the oven to 450°F.

Line a 9 x 9-inch baking pan with foil.

Put the granola in a large bowl.

In a saucepan, combine the butter, brown sugar, and honey. Mix and stir on low heat until it's smooth and the sugar has dissolved.

Pour the butter mixture over the granola and mix well.

Pack down this mixture into the foil-lined 9 x 9-inch square baking pan.

Bake for about 6 to 8 minutes. It will be brown and bubbly.

Cool completely on a wire rack and then invert the pan onto a cutting board.

Remove the pan and the foil.

Cut the granola slab into bars or bite-size pieces.

Store this snack in zip-top plastic bags in your refrigerator to be grabbed as you go out the door.

Jan's Saddlebag Trail Mix

MAKES 8 CUPS

Let us introduce you to Jan Shipman and her trail buddy, Bull, a mini Australian Shepherd with the heart of a lion. Jan can be found in almost any weather out on the trail on a good horse she is training, with Bull riding on the saddle behind her. They cover a lot of territory together. We asked Jan what she puts into her saddlebags for those long rides and this is what she sent me. It's really good! And best of all? She can feed it to Bull, too.

6 cups old-fashioned oats

2 cups shredded unsweetened coconut

6 cups pecan halves

⅓ cup canola oil

½ cup brown sugar

½ cup crunchy peanut butter

½ cup honey

2 teaspoons ground cinnamon

1 teaspoon vanilla extract

Preheat the oven to 325°F.

Prepare a large, shallow baking pan with foil.

In a large mixing bowl, combine the oats, shredded coconut, and the pecan halves.

In a small saucepan, combine the canola oil, brown sugar, peanut butter, honey, cinnamon, and vanilla. Heat over medium, stirring it all together until smooth.

Then pour the liquid over the oat mixture and stir until it's well combined.

Spread this mixture as evenly as you can into the prepared pan.

Bake until browned, about 50 minutes, stirring it every 10 minutes with a flat spoon or spatula.

Cool the mixture on a wire rack. When it is completely cool, stir it all up again.

You can store this for 2 weeks in an airtight container. Put as much as you like in a zip-top plastic bag to take on your trail ride.

Credit: Jan Shipman

Lorrie's Saddlebag Pies

MAKES 12 PIES

You can go many more miles on the trail with something hearty in your belly. Cowgirl Lorrie Turner shared this marvelous hand pie recipe her mother used to make.

"The ranch hands could put these meat pies in the saddlebags and have something to tide them over before lunch or dinner. My mom would make these pies for my dad to take on his long hunting trips. He could put a couple in his pack (wrapped in wax paper) and go out looking for his elk or deer. I used to make them for my boys because they were something I could make ahead of time and keep in the fridge. All they had to do was warm them up in the microwave or eat them cold."

Lorrie has a wonderful shortcut to making all that dough.

2 cans Pillsbury Grands!™ Biscuits
3 tablespoons butter, divided
1 cup chopped sweet onion
2 cups chopped mushrooms (cremini are best but any fresh mushroom will do)
2 cups chopped green cabbage
1 teaspoon salt
1 teaspoon pepper
1 pound ground beef
3 tablespoons Worcestershire sauce
2 tablespoons sweet hot deli mustard
¼ teaspoon red pepper flakes (optional)
1 cup grated sharp cheddar cheese

Melt 2 tablespoons of the butter in a cast iron skillet or Dutch oven.

Sauté the onions, mushrooms, and cabbage until the onions are translucent. Season with the salt and pepper.

Remove from the pan with a slotted spoon and set aside on a paper towel.

Sauté the ground beef until it is completely cooked. Lorrie seasons her ground beef with salt, pepper, ground garlic, and a pinch of brown sugar, to taste. Drain off the excess fat and moisture.

Stir in the Worcestershire sauce, mustard, red pepper flakes, and the onion-cabbage mixture and stir well to combine.

Preheat the oven to 375°F.

Take one biscuit square at a time and roll it out thin, approximately 5 inches in diameter.

Put a heaping teaspoon of shredded cheese and about 2 tablespoons of the meat mixture in the center of the dough.

Fold the dough over, pinching the edges together to seal. Using a fork, pierce the top to allow steam to escape while cooking. Place the pie on a cookie sheet.

Continue rolling, filling, pinching, and piercing the remaining pies and placing them on the cookie sheet.

Melt the remaining 1 tablespoon of butter and brush the tops of the pies.

Bake for 20 to 25 minutes until they are browned nicely.

Cool on a wire rack.

These pies can be frozen, and are easily reheated in a microwave or a Dutch oven over some hot coals if you are camping. You can store them in your saddlebags, wrapped in wax paper like Lorrie's dad did for a trail lunch. They are wonderful cold!

ELMA WASHBURN, COWGIRL COOK

Lorrie shares this memory about her mother, Elma Washburn: "My mom and dad worked a ranch in Helena, Montana, back in the 1940s. Dad worked the cattle and Mom fed all the ranch hands. I think this is where she got into the habit of cooking the same meal every week on certain days. She never strayed off course, probably just easier that way with seven kids in the house. (I was one of them—four girls and three boys!) Monday was her bread making day and she would make enough bread dough to get in all her loaves for the week, plus cinnamon rolls, hand pies, and chicken and dumplings for dinner. We always knew what day it was based on our meal.

"Mom loved gardening and her garden sustained us through the winter. She grew and canned everything from green beans, carrots, stewed tomatoes, corn, zucchini relish, dill pickles, sweet pickles, butter pickles, pumpkin for pies, apple pie filling, and applesauce. Our dirt cellar had everything we needed like potatoes and onions that we grew and we rarely went to the store. We raised all our food except for what Dad, Grandpa, and the boys hunted. We ate what we raised and grew ourselves."

And we can only add that this pretty lady (and Lorrie resembles her 100 percent in every way) has become one of my idols.

Credit: Courtesy of Lorrie Turner

Pack Mule Cookies

MAKES ABOUT 2 DOZEN COOKIES

We named these Pack Mule Cookies because you can load everything and anything into this basic cookie recipe and they will never balk, falter, or fail. They are stout and can travel with you wherever you are going. Unlike mules, however, these freeze well.

1½ cups sugar
⅔ cup shortening
2 large eggs
½ teaspoon salt
2 teaspoons vanilla extract
1 teaspoon nutmeg
2½ cups all-purpose flour
1 teaspoon baking soda
1 cup old-fashioned oats
½ cup dried cranberries (optional)
¼ cup fresh orange peel (optional)

Preheat the oven to 375°F.

Grease a baking pan or cookie sheet.

In a large bowl, cream together the wet ingredients and spices (sugar through nutmeg). Then stir in the flour, baking soda, and oats.

Now add the "mules." We used cranberries and orange peel, but other suggested additions are chocolate chips, diced raw apple, ½ cup chopped nuts, diced dried dates, and raisins. The possibilities are endless!

Mix all this together and drop large spoonfuls of dough onto a greased baking pan.

Use the back of the spoon to press them all down to a uniform size.

Bake for 8 to 10 minutes. They should not get too brown.

Cool on a wire rack and place as many as you want in zip-top bags for your trail snack or a freezer-safe container for later.

Chapter 3

PICNIC DISHES AND MAKE-AHEAD LUNCHES

COWGIRL PICNIC

This image is a great favorite of ours for quite a few reasons, not the least of which is that they are having a picnic. We think the lower two are sisters as they resemble one another. Their "Mexican-style" sombreros tell us they are somewhere in the Southwest. They are using old coffee cans as their lunch pails and we love the loaf of bread the upper girl is holding. See that glass bottle of milk? And what's in that bowl?

Credit: Author's Collection

Already Wilted Salad

SERVES 4

There is no need to worry about this salad staying fresh. Why? Because it's already wilted and also very, very good. It's an old-time recipe and still a good one!

6 strips bacon
¼ cup diced green onions
½ cup white vinegar
4 teaspoons sugar
Salt, to taste
8 cups leaf lettuce of your choice, torn
    into bite-size pieces

Cook the bacon in a skillet until crispy, then remove and let it drain over paper towels to absorb the grease. When the bacon is cool, crumble it up with your fingers.

Add the onions to the drippings in the pan and cook them until they are tender.

Add in the vinegar and the sugar, then add the salt and the bacon. Cook and stir until it's boiling.

Place the lettuce in a serving bowl and pour the hot dressing over the lettuce and toss. It wilts!

Let cool completely before serving. This keeps well in a storage container with a tight-fitting lid.

When you get to the picnic or potluck, garnish with sliced hard-boiled eggs and/or thinly sliced radishes (also kept in a storage container and kept cool).

Bacon, Tomato, and Cheese Hand Pies

MAKES 8 PIES

Hand pies are always a favorite no matter if they are sweet or savory. They are good to take along on a picnic or on a camping trip because they travel well and heat up easily, if you decide to heat them up before you enjoy them, by wrapping them individually in foil and placing them on the grill. You can get creative and substitute ingredients or add others to this recipe if you want and they will be delish no matter what you decide to include! What follows is our version that can be good for a picnic lunch or a dinner. We like them with the Cowgirl Baked Beans (see page 63) and Watermelon and Tomato Summer Salad (see page 107).

2 ready-made frozen pie crusts, thawed in the refrigerator for 1–2 days
1 tablespoon butter
3 ounces (⅓ cup) fully cooked bacon, cut into small pieces (precooked ham works well, too)
¾ cup diced sweet onion
1 cup frozen shredded hash brown potatoes, thawed
⅓ cup seeded and diced fresh tomato
2–3 tablespoons sour cream
½ cup shredded cheddar cheese
Salt and pepper, to taste
1 egg, whisked lightly for the egg wash

Preheat the oven to 400°F and move a rack to the middle of the oven.

Line a cookie sheet with parchment paper.

Using a glass or a cup that measures about 5 inches in diameter, cut the pie crusts into eight rounds. (**Cowgirl tip:** Flour the rim of the glass or cup before pressing into the dough.)

Cover the crust with plastic and put it back in the refrigerator while you prepare the filling.

In a medium fry pan, melt the butter and refry the bacon briefly on medium heat for 2 to 3 minutes to re-crisp. Add the onions and cook with the bacon until translucent, about 3 minutes.

Add the potatoes and tomatoes and continue to cook this mix for 5 minutes. Set this mixture aside and let it cool to room temperature.

When it is cool, add the sour cream, cheddar cheese, salt, and pepper, and stir well. The mix should stay together well—add a little more sour cream if needed.

Retrieve the pie rounds from the refrigerator and begin the assembly process one hand pie at a time. Brush each pie round completely with the whisked egg wash and then place a heaping tablespoon on half of each pie round. Make sure you are leaving enough of the edge to fold the doughover the filling and press down to seal each pie with your fingers. Then take a fork and press down on the edge to decoratively secure your seal. You don't want any of the filling to leak out of your pies!

When they are all assembled, place the pies on the parchment-lined cookie sheet, and brush the tops with the remaining egg wash.

Bake until golden brown, about 30 minutes.

Cool completely before setting out on your picnic. They keep well in a plastic container.

PERRY PARK PICNIC

What a lovely scene this is. Four women (unidentified but we bet one is the mother of the child) and little Doug Ellis have driven their buggy to this spot to enjoy a light lunch in beautiful Perry Park, Colorado. The Perry Park area was originally inhabited by the Ute, Kiowa, Arapaho, and Cheyenne tribes. It was not settled by American immigrants until the 1858 Pike's Peak Gold Rush and is located near present-day Colorado Springs, Colorado.

The ladies are, of course, wearing their hats. Note that they have removed the buggy seat for two of the ladies to sit on, while the others are content to be on a blanket and the horses are tied, still harnessed, to the tree to rest before the journey home again. Looks to us like they brought sandwiches and a metal cooler to keep the tea cold.

Cream Cheese, Ham, and Pickle Roll-Up

MAKES 5 ROLL-UPS

Yum! That was the exact word spoken when we handed our friend this roll-up on a spur-of-the-moment picnic. Very easy to prepare; we kept everything chilled in our backpack before eating.

Pinch of garlic powder (more if you wish)
8 ounces softened cream cheese
5 (6-inch) tortillas
½ pound sliced ham
5 crunchy dill pickles, cut into spears

Mix the garlic powder into the cream cheese until well incorporated.

To assemble, spread the cream cheese mixture on a tortilla. Put one or two slices of ham onto the cream cheese. Put a pickle spear on top of the ham and roll it up. Repeat with the remaining tortillas.

Wrap tightly in plastic wrap and keep cool in a container.

Curried Chicken Salad Wrap

MAKES 24 WRAPS

Add a bit of spice to your trail ride with this delicious recipe from Lorrie Turner. She really knows her way around a wrap. This would be a great picnic sandwich, too! We also like that this is possibly the easiest recipe to cut in half if you don't want to make very many.

4 cooked chicken breasts, cut into bite-size pieces

2 Granny Smith apples, peeled and chopped into bite-size pieces

2 cups red grapes, washed and sliced in half

2 cups shredded sharp cheddar cheese

2 cups thinly chopped celery, strings removed

2 cups pecan pieces

2 cups mayonnaise

¼ cup curry powder (give or take a little more or less depending on your tastes)

1 package spinach tortillas (or whatever tortillas you like)

Green leaf lettuce or chopped salad (optional)

Prepare and combine the first six ingredients in a large bowl (chicken through pecans).

In a separate bowl, mix together the mayonnaise and curry powder.

Add the dressing to your salad ingredients and combine until everything is thoroughly coated.

When you are ready to make the wraps, take each tortilla, add the optional green leaf lettuce or the chopped salad (about 2 handfuls), and top with the Curried Chicken Salad.

Roll the tortillas up, wrap in wax paper or sandwich bags, and keep in your refrigerator until you are ready to hit the trail or leave for your picnic. Just make sure to keep this cool wherever it goes.

Devilishly Good Ham and Chicken Sandwich

MAKES 4 SANDWICHES

Ham and chicken get cozy with olives for a great, hearty picnic sandwich.

8 slices thick sourdough bread, buttered
1 cup finely chopped cooked ham
1 cup finely chopped cooked chicken
½ cup pitted green olives, chopped (We like the pimento stuffed ones! They add a little color, as well as taste.)
1 cup mayonnaise
Salt and pepper, to taste

Combine all the ingredients in a medium-size bowl.

Spread this mixture over the buttered bread and cut the sandwich in half.

Wrap lightly in wax paper and keep this sandwich cool as a cucumber in an insulated sandwich carrier!

Green Olive and Cheese Sandwich Spread

MAKES 2 CUPS

When we were little girls, a big "treat" was when our mother bought the pimento cheese spread that came in a small, clear glass jar. She would make us sandwiches with this spread and we loved them. They were a nice change from PB&J, as well as bologna. (She washed and rinsed the empty glasses and those became our "juice glasses.") Recently, we wondered if we could re-create that wonderful sandwich, so we did! But, of course, we added our own touch to it. We think you will like this. It also makes a great spread for crackers!

1½ cups grated sharp cheddar cheese, softened

½ cup cream cheese, softened

½ cup green olives stuffed with pimentos, chopped (feel free to add more)

¼ cup mayonnaise

1 tablespoon Worcestershire sauce (or to taste)

Combine all the ingredients in a bowl and mix together until smooth. (We softened the cheeses by putting them in the microwave on low for a minute or so.) We liked it on white bread, with butter and a few bread and butter pickles, cherry tomatoes from the garden, and a few more green olives stuffed with pimentos. Keep this mix in an airtight container in the refrigerator. It will keep for up to 2 weeks. Let it "warm" if you are serving it as a spread for crackers.

Hawaii Calls Sandwich

SERVES 1

Jill remembers a VERY wet "trail ride" in the Columbia Gorge on a very green, young horse and actually crossing the Columbia River in shallow water to a sandbar that became an island. This is the sandwich she made for her saddlebags. Sitting on a (wet) log, she could almost hear the surf off Oahu—well, to be honest, there were waves on the Columbia River! And it was raining hard, too. But these flavors reminded her of a warmer place, as she wondered, "Whose idea was this anyway?"

2 slices thick sourdough bread
Butter (for spreading)
1 can deviled ham spread
1 tablespoon cream cheese, softened
   (whipped cream cheese works
   very well)
1 tablespoon drained crushed
   pineapple

Butter one slice of bread and spread the deviled ham over it. Then spread the cream cheese on the other slice of bread.

Add the pineapple over the cream cheese.

Press the slices together and push down a bit to meld them.

Cut the sandwich in half and wrap well in wax paper.

Keep cool in your backpack or saddlebag.

Aloha!

No Mayo Red Potato Salad

SERVES 4-6

This is a recipe that Robin has had for many years. It was a staple at her favorite restaurant and she decided to try to re-create this potato salad. She says she has come pretty close. It is lighter than potato salad made with mayonnaise, which also means it won't spoil as fast. We recommend pairing this with burgers or Baby Back Ribs (see recipe on page 57).

2 pounds red potatoes, cut into ½-inch cubes
¼ cup chopped parsley
¼ cup chopped green onions
½ cup black olives, cut in half
½ cup chopped celery
2 tablespoons fresh dill or ½ tablespoon dried
¼ cup red wine vinegar
½ cup olive oil
Salt and pepper, to taste
Crumbled bacon (optional)

Cover the cut potatoes in a medium saucepan in cold water and salt them generously. (**Cowgirl tip:** Put cut potatoes in salted water to keep them from browning until you are ready to boil.) Bring the potatoes to a boil and then lower the heat to medium and let them cook 10 to 15 minutes. Smaller cubes of potatoes will require less time, and larger cubes more. Drain the potatoes and set them aside to cool.

Toss the parsley, green onions, black olives, celery, and dill together and then add the cooled potatoes and gently combine.

In a small bowl whisk the red wine vinegar and olive oil together and pour the dressing on the potato mixture. Gently toss until well combined. Salt and pepper to taste and garnish with the bacon if you want.

Picnic Mushrooms

MAKES 8 MUSHROOMS

Ever wonder what the British take on a picnic? We did, too. Thanks to cowgirl Gail James, who lives "across the pond" and who spent a very thrilling month up on the High Plateau of Central Washington State with horses and cattle and dogs, for sharing this recipe. This is a great treat in our view and you don't have to hunt for the mushrooms—another bonus. We think these would also be good served as a hot side dish. Gail says, "These are taken cold to the picnic spot."

8 flat mushrooms, like portobellos
Olive oil (for brushing mushrooms)
4 small cherry tomatoes, chopped
1 cup blue cheese crumbles

Preheat oven to 350°F.

Remove the stems from the mushrooms, then clean them and brush with olive oil.

Mix the tomatoes and blue cheese together in a bowl.

Fill each mushroom with the tomato and blue cheese mixture.

Place the mushrooms on a baking sheet lined with parchment paper and bake for about 20 minutes.

Other filling options could include: Parmesan cheese; the mushroom stems, chopped and sautéed in butter; or Mexican three cheese.

One of our tasters suggested adding bacon bits on top of any of these and we couldn't agree more.

Rod's Lunch

SERVES 1

Once in a blue moon, we include a cowboy's recipe in our books. Rod Castelda is not a cowboy at all, but he fills the bill in so many other ways—he grew up in a small town in Washington State in a hard-working family with numerous siblings. There were plenty of orchards to keep a boy busy picking peaches and earning money all summer and that's what Rod did. Eventually, he saved enough to go to college. We were talking about this book and he said, shyly, "I don't suppose you would be interested in what sandwich I ate every day as a boy?" He added, "I still like them."

Here it is. And we have to admit, we like them, too. A LOT.

2 slices white bread
Yellow mustard
1 tablespoon brown sugar
1 thick slab Spam

Spread the yellow mustard (no cheating and substituting Dijon) on one slice of bread.

Sprinkle as much brown sugar over the mustard as you like.

Place a slab of Spam as thick or as thin as you want on top of the mustard and brown sugar.

Place the remaining slice of bread on top and press down hard.

Wrap tightly in wax paper (which you will save for tomorrow's sandwich) and then use a rubber band.

Put in your back pocket.

TEDDY BEARS' PICNIC—RETHOUGHT

As we mentioned in A Note from the Authors, our mother told us (and we still believe this) that the Teddy Bears' Picnic featured peanut butter and honey sandwiches on white bread with the crusts cut off. We still love them. But there are a number of other ways to have a peanut butter sandwich. The added bonus is that peanut butter is high in fiber and packed with protein—a perfect trail partner ingredient.

Let us count the ways for you:

1. Try a different nut butter.

PB might the most popular protein-packed sandwich spread, but it's not the only one sold in grocery stores. You'll probably find almond, cashew, and hazelnut butters at your local supermarket, and specialty stores carry even more varieties, like sunflower and pumpkin seed butters, Brazil nut butter, and pistachio butter. Each one boasts unique health properties, and—more importantly—they provide your sandwich with new, distinct flavors without sacrificing the creamy texture you love.

2. Experiment with different jams.

Grape jelly is the go-to fruit spread for PB&Js, but other sweet preserves might taste just as good (if not better) when paired with nut butters. Try strawberry, raspberry, red plum jam, mango, blackberry, blueberry, and even boysenberry. And if you're feeling really adventurous, you can opt for a savory spread, like Jammy Bacon (see page 64).

3. Toast it, grill it, or fry it.

No one ever said a peanut butter sandwich is best served cold. Try grilling it, frying it, cooking it in a panini press, or toasting it in the oven.

4. Spice it up.

Raid your spice cabinet and sprinkle a pinch of cinnamon, pumpkin pie spice, apple pie spice, nutmeg, cloves, or cardamom over your peanut butter. Looking for more of a kick? Opt for cayenne pepper and chili powder.

5. Go double-decker.

Consider making yourself a double-decker PB&J. Take three pieces of bread, and cover two with jelly and one with PB. Place the PB-covered bread slice sticky-side down on top of one of the jelly-covered slices, and add more peanut butter to its other side. Place the second jelly-covered slice on top, cut it in half, and voila!

6. Try different breads.

Skip the white sandwich bread and opt for baguettes, sourdough, whole grains, English muffins, and even tortillas (try rolling them up like burritos).

7. Swap jelly for fruit.

Looking to cut down on added sugars? Swap sweet spreads out for fresh fruits like grapes, blueberries, and strawberries. (If you miss the texture of jelly, try sautéing the fruits before putting them into your sandwich.)

8. Mash it up.

Instead of jelly, try mashed banana—and you can pan fry this sandwich to a golden brown (lightly butter the bread before frying).

9. How about a Thai PB?

Make yourself a Thai-inspired sandwich by covering whole-grain bread with peanut butter, shredded rotisserie chicken, sliced cucumbers, shredded carrots, chopped red onions, and hot sauce.

10. And finally, drizzle your PB with honey.

A peanut butter sandwich made on whole wheat bread and drizzled with honey is filled with healthy complex carbs, it's simple to make, and Winnie the Pooh, who ate nothing but honey, would be delighted!

Vegetarian's Delight Sandwich

MAKES 2 SANDWICHES

We believe this is a sandwich you could share a little of with your horse! Our horses would gobble this up.

1 cup chopped celery, strings removed
1 cup peeled and chopped cucumber
¼ cup chopped sweet onion
  (Bermudas are quite good!)
6 stuffed green olives, chopped
¼ cup sprouts or seeded and chopped
  green pepper
4 tablespoons mayonnaise
Butter (for spreading)
4 slices thick bread (a hearty whole
  wheat is terrific)

Add the vegetables to a bowl and stir in mayonnaise. Mix until everything is well-covered and thick enough to spread.

Butter each slice of bread, then add a generous scoop of the vegetable-mayonnaise spread to each sandwich.

Cut the sandwich in half and wrap well, then keep cool in your picnic basket or saddlebag.

Optional additions to top off the spread: sliced avocado, sliced red radishes, or sliced heirloom tomatoes.

Chapter 4

WHEN THE SUN SINKS IN THE WEST— CAMPFIRE COOKING AND GRILLING

Baby Back Ribs

SERVES 4

Would we rib you? Never! Who doesn't like great ribs? We think this is a dandy way to cook baby backs with little fuss and the meat falls right off the bone. There is one drawback—just one. You have to wait about 1 hour and 15 minutes before you can enjoy them. We think the Corny Bacon Foil Wraps (see page 61) are a great accompaniment because they cook right alongside the ribs.

2 racks baby back ribs, about 2 pounds each
1 cup BBQ sauce (we suggest June's Best BBQ, see page 75)
Salt and pepper, to taste
Garlic powder, to taste

Start your grill or campfire, making sure the cooking racks are clean.

Cut the baby backs in half to create four servings (about 1 pound per person).

Using 18-inch-wide heavy-duty foil, put one serving of ribs onto its own piece of foil and season it evenly over the top with the salt, pepper, and garlic powder.

Now spread about ¼ cup of BBQ sauce on top of the rack, spreading it evenly.

Close up the foil packet tightly—you want steam to build up in there with no leaking. Repeat with the other three portions of ribs.

Place the foil-wrapped ribs on the grill over a medium flame (or other heat source) and cook for about 1 hour.

Turn them over now and then being careful not to pierce the foil.

Remove the packets and let them rest for about 10 minutes. Then carefully open the packets and remove the ribs. Return them to the grill, bone-side down, and let them sizzle and char lightly, turning them and basting them with a little more BBQ sauce.

Remove them from the grill onto a serving plate and let them rest again so that the juices go back into the meat. Now you can cut them into individual pieces (this is optional) and go to town! Get out plenty of napkins!

Credit: GettyImages/GMVozd

Camp Kabobs

SERVES 4 HUNGRY CAMPERS

Cowgirl Janice Gilbertson loves horse camping. She took a trip to Banff National Park in Canada and spent several days on the trail enjoying the beautiful wilderness and being spoiled by the camp cook for breakfast, lunch, and dinner.

In praise of these kabobs, Janice says: "These are good because you can make them up at home and freeze them in zip-lock bags. If you are camping with an ice chest, they can keep for several days. If you are packing, these are a great first-night meal."

4 skewers

2 chicken breasts, boned, or 1 pound beef stew meat, cut into chunks

2 cups broccoli florets

1 red or sweet onion, roughly chopped

1 zucchini squash, thickly sliced

2 carrots, thickly sliced

8 brussels sprouts, halved

8 red potatoes, halved

Lemon pepper or other seasoning, to taste

After preparing all the ingredients, skewer the meat and (any or all) vegetables onto individual wooden kabob sticks in an alternating pattern. Generously sprinkle the kabobs with lemon pepper or your favorite seasoning, or brush with teriyaki sauce (they will marinate in the zip-top bag). Store in the fridge or a cooler until ready to cook.

Lay the kabobs on the grill over a good fire—no flames, just hot coals. Turn them once or twice so they are evenly cooked.

Place the skewers on a paper plate, and "zip off" the meat and vegetables.

Campout Country Fair Fry Bread

MAKES 8 ROLLS

This is easy and fun to do in your cast iron skillet over a campfire. Or, in your kitchen on the stove. Very versatile, this bread is a great accompaniment to breakfast when filled with butter and jam and rolled, or lunch with a hot dog rolled inside (don't forget the ketchup!), or with dinner as the starch to go with the grilled steak, chicken, or chops, and maybe Corny Bacon Foil Wraps (see recipe page 61).

2 cups all-purpose flour
2½ teaspoons baking powder
1 teaspoon salt
1 cup warm water
3 cups vegetable oil

In a large bowl, combine the flour, baking powder, and salt. If you are going camping, put these dry ingredients into a secure 1-gallon zip-top bag.

Add the warm water (right into the bag if you are camping) and mix, using a fork, until a dough forms.

Turn the dough out onto a lightly floured surface and knead for 5 minutes, then transfer to a clean bowl and cover tightly in plastic wrap. Let the dough rest for 10 minutes.

Divide the dough into eight equal sections by pinching off golf ball–size balls of dough. Pat and roll out the dough balls into roughly 6-inch discs on a lightly floured surface. Keep them covered with plastic wrap while you prepare to fry them.

Heat the oil in a large skillet or frying pan over medium heat (or fire) for about 5 minutes until the oil temperature reaches between 350 and 360°F. Working in batches, fry each disc in the hot oil until the dough is golden brown on one side, then carefully flip with tongs and fry on the other side.

Set the bread on a paper towel to drain the oil off and keep warm in the oven or in foil by the fire to stay hot while the other fry breads are cooked.

For a fry bread cinnamon roll-up, combine equal parts cinnamon and sugar. Sprinkle over the warm bread. Great for breakfast or dessert.

Corny Bacon Foil Wraps

MAKES 4 WRAPS

Bacon makes everything better. Why not corn on the cob? Who thought of this? We are giving you the basic idea and you can play with this all you want by adding toppings like jalapenos (spicy!) or blue cheese crumbles (pretty darn good). These make a great side dish for grilled meat.

4 ears corn
8 slices bacon
Salt and pepper, to taste
Heavy-duty aluminum foil

Remove the leaves and silk from the corn.

Wrap two slices of uncooked bacon around each ear of corn. Now put each bacon-wrapped ear of corn on a piece of foil, sprinkle a little salt and pepper on each, and then close the foil and twist the ends tightly.

Grill over the fire for about 20 minutes turning every 5 minutes.

Remove the foil packets from the grill and open each package. Put the bacon-wrapped corn directly on the grill for a couple of minutes to crisp the bacon, watching carefully so it doesn't burn.

If you're at home, you can also cook these in your oven at 375°F for 30 minutes.

Cowgirl Baked Beans

SERVES 4-6

We don't think grilling outdoors is complete without a good pot of beans bubbling alongside whatever you decide to serve. The pineapple adds a nice zing to these sweet, tasty beans that are a cinch to throw together.

1 tablespoon vegetable oil or butter
1 cup diced sweet onion
1 (28-ounce) can baked beans
½ cup canned pineapple chunks
3 tablespoons ketchup
1 teaspoon prepared yellow mustard
1 tablespoon molasses
Cooked bacon pieces (optional, for garnish)

In a medium saucepan add the oil and sauté the onions until they are slightly brown. Then add the remaining ingredients except the bacon and bring to a boil. Reduce the heat and simmer for about 30 minutes, stirring frequently.

Serve with your favorite BBQ as a side dish and feel free to sprinkle the crispy, cooked bacon pieces on top as a garnish for extra taste and crunch!

Cowgirl Jill's Campfire Jammy Bacon

MAKES ABOUT 2 CUPS

We understand that Martha Stewart came up with this delicious idea, but, as we all know, she is not a cowgirl. So we took the initial idea and made it suitable for cowgirls. You can spread this on toast, crackers, a baked potato, a burger or—let's not kid ourselves—eat it straight off the spoon for a bacon high!

1 pound good, uncooked bacon, cut into ½-inch pieces
1 sweet onion, very finely chopped
4 garlic cloves, finely chopped
¾ cup strong black coffee (you can substitute black tea if you wish)
½ cup dark brown sugar
¼ cup maple syrup
2 tablespoons liquid smoke
¼ cup whiskey (and we all know that is Pendleton Whisky, don't we?!)

In a medium frying pan over medium heat, cook the bacon until just browning. Using a slotted spoon, put the bacon bits on a paper towel to drain, but reserve about a tablespoon of bacon fat in the pan.

Reduce heat to medium-low. Add the onion and garlic to the bacon fat and cook, stirring often, until the onion and garlic are caramelized. This takes about 15 minutes.

Stir in the coffee (or tea), brown sugar, maple syrup, liquid smoke, and whiskey. Now add the cooked bacon.

Bring mixture up to a boil and then transfer it into a Crock-Pot on low for about 7 hours, or until it gets "jammy."

Let the jam cool. Transfer it to a blender or a food processor and pulse it until it is smooth—it will be like blackberry jam.

Store in the icebox in tightly sealed and sterilized glass jars. Keeps for 4 weeks.

CAST IRON TIPS AND MORE

When you buy a cast iron skillet, or a Dutch oven, or anything else made of cast iron, you are buying an item that will serve you well. The more you use your cast iron, the better. Clean the cast iron after every use, using only warm water while the iron is still warm. A coarse bristled brush will clean the bits of food left in the iron. We repeat—use only warm water. NO SOAP. Never, ever, pinky-swear, put your cast iron in the dishwasher! Always dry the iron with paper towels or a soft cloth.

Robin is using the Dutch oven that belonged to our mother for some of the recipes in this book. Jill bought a new one and seasoned it.

To season your cast iron, give it a light coating of vegetable oil. Think of it as moisturizer for your skin. Pays off in the long run!

When you are storing your cast iron, put a paper towel between the lid and the pot to create airflow and avoid rust. You can also put a little dry rice on the bottom to absorb any moisture.

If you find a piece of cast iron in a garage sale, and it is really cheap because it is rusty, buy it and then do this: Rub the iron with steel wool. Really rub it well! Then wash it with warm water and, JUST THIS ONCE, a mild dish soap. Dry it well! Then rub it with vegetable oil. Inside, outside, on the handle, everywhere. Then wipe away the excess. Finally, bake the iron in a 400°F oven for about an hour. Place it upside down on the lowest rack that has been lined with foil. You may have to repeat the oiling and baking several times to get the desired glossy nonstick sheen so loved by cast iron fans.

Dutch Oven Chicken Pot Pie

MAKES 1 POT PIE

Nothing warms you up after a day of riding or hiking and prepares you for sleeping under the stars more than this chicken pot pie dish! Many thanks to cowgirl Lorrie Turner for sharing yet another recipe that we've eaten and always want seconds! This meal is ridiculously easy to make. We think the hardest part might be making the fire and waiting for it to burn to coals.

1 large roasted chicken (**Cowgirl tip:** Buy one already roasted and ready from the grocery store.)

2 carrots, peeled and chopped into bite-size pieces

1 sweet potato, peeled and chopped into bite-size pieces

1 onion, peeled and chopped

1 tablespoon red pepper flakes

1 teaspoon ground thyme

1 teaspoon ground sage

1 teaspoon garlic powder

1 tablespoon salt

1 tablespoon pepper

2 tablespoons olive oil

2 tablespoons butter

1 (10.5-ounce) can cream of chicken soup

1 cup chicken broth

½ cup milk (dried milk can be used)

1 cup frozen sweet peas

1 cup grated cheddar cheese

1 small box of Bisquick

½ cup skim milk

Note: We recommend prepping the ingredients at home and packing them for the campsite.

Remove the skin and bones from the roasted chicken and chop meat into bite-size pieces.

Pour the reserved chicken juice from the roasting pan over the chopped chicken to keep it from drying out. (If you buy pre-cooked chicken, tear the chicken into bite-size pieces, discarding the skin and bones, and store in a zip-top bag.) Let it cool and then store in a zip-top bag.

Chop all the vegetables (except the peas) and put them in another large zip-top bag. (Do not add peas yet as they are the last to go in the pie.)

Add the dry seasonings, olive oil, and butter to your vegetable bag and close. Pack the remaining ingredients together with all of the above into a plastic "tote" so your meal is all together in one container. (**Cowgirl tip:** Put all this into the Dutch oven.) Be sure to add a bag of ice or cold packs to keep everything cold until you are ready to cook.

Start your fire about 15 minutes before you plan to cook, so the flames have died down, leaving hot coals.

Place your Dutch oven on the hot coals. Then pour in your bag of vegetable mix into the pot. Cook on the coals for 10 to 15 minutes, stirring to make sure the vegetables aren't burning and allowing enough time for the onions to sweat and create a little moisture.

Add the chopped chicken to the Dutch oven and give that a good stir. Then add in the soup, broth, and milk. Stir until combined.

Next layer on the frozen peas and cheddar cheese. Put the lid on the oven and let it cook while you prepare your biscuits.

Follow the directions on the Bisquick box to make about 6 to 8 drop biscuits. (Depending on how many bodies are around the campfire, you want enough biscuits that everyone gets one with their chicken pot pie.)

Using a towel or a hot pad, remove the lid from the Dutch oven and give the chicken and vegetable mix one more good stir. Drop heaping spoonfuls of the biscuit batter onto the pie mixture, first around the edges then one in the middle.

Put the lid back on the Dutch oven and cook for 30 minutes or until your biscuits are done, nicely browned around the edges and the tops.

Credit: GettyImages/LauriPatterson

Grilled Potato Planks

SERVES 4

This dish couldn't be easier to prepare and is a perfect accompaniment to the steak, chicken, or ribs you are grilling.

3 tablespoons olive oil
1 clove garlic, minced
2 teaspoons finely chopped fresh
  rosemary
½ teaspoon salt
4 large yellow potatoes, peeled and
  cut into ½-inch slices

Start your fire to burn down to hot coals or reheat the grill.

Combine the oil, garlic, rosemary, and salt in a dish.

Put the potato slices in the dish with the oil, garlic, rosemary, and salt and turn them until they are well-coated.

Grill the potatoes for about 8 minutes, turning once or twice. Continue grilling 10 minutes longer or until cooked through.

Remove from grill and serve.

COOKING IN THE GREAT OUTDOORS

Cooking outdoors is nothing new and camp kitchens come in all shapes and sizes—from ice chests and saddlebags, to chuck wagons with portable pantries. This photograph, taken by conservationist J. Stokely Ligon on his survey trip through San Mateo, New Mexico, in 1912, shows the chuck box from a chuck wagon set up and ready for use. You can see cans, boxes, and bags of food with condiments, cooking kettle, and frying pan.

Credit: The Denver Public Library, Western History Collection, CONS92-2017-26

Hearty Dutch Oven Nachos

SERVES 4 HUNGRY CAMPERS

Our erstwhile guide, Lauralee Northcott, shares this great dinner recipe from her book, A Cowgirl's Life in the Mountains, *and we highly recommend it! Enjoy this meal following a ride up the Windigo Trail and back again.*

1 pound lean ground beef

2 tablespoons taco seasoning

1 large bag tortilla chips

1 (4-ounce) can green chilies, diced

1 (6-ounce) can black olives, sliced

2 cups shredded Monterey Jack and cheddar cheese

1 cup sour cream

2 cups mild salsa

Get your campfire going or preheat your oven to 350°F.

Brown the ground beef with the taco seasoning in your cast iron skillet. Set aside and let cool.

Fill your Dutch oven about halfway up with the chips. Top with half the portion of the ground beef, diced chiles, olives, and cheese.

Add another layer of chips, but don't overfill—you will want to get the top on that Dutch oven! Add the remaining half of the beef, chiles, olives, and cheese.

Place the Dutch oven onto the grill over the hot coals. Put the lid on the Dutch oven, and shovel hot coals right onto the top. Let this cook for about 45 minutes. If you are using an oven, bake for 45 minutes.

Serve in bowls with the sour cream and salsa on the side.

In a Pinch Chili and Tamales

SERVES 2

When traveling in an RV for a long distance (maybe to a horse show in another state?), it isn't always easy to set up camp and then come up with something easy, quick, and good for dinner. However, in a pinch, if you have a can of chili and a can of tamales, some green onions, and cheddar cheese, you can do this tasty bake in just 30 minutes. This is a "go-to" recipe that is really good served with crackers and a salad if you have the strength!

1 (15-ounce) can beef tamales
1 (15-ounce) can beef chili with beans
2 or more green onions, chopped
Cheddar cheese, grated (for topping)

Preheat the oven to 350°F, or prepare the grill or the fire, letting the flames go down to a nice glow.

In a medium saucepan or any oven-safe pan, unwrap the tamales and place them on the bottom of the pan. Now open the can of chili and spread on top of the tamales. Then sprinkle the green onions and as much of the cheddar cheese as you like (we think more is better) over the chili.

Heat this in the pan over the camp stove, or in the oven, but put the top on the pan and simmer for 30 minutes until it is bubbling and the cheese has melted.

This can be reheated in a preheated 350°F oven for 30 minutes.

June's Best BBQ Sauce

MAKES 4 CUPS

Robin says, "This is a recipe from my husband Jim's mother that I have had for nearly forty years. It was scratched out on a memo pad. It's a classic and better than anything store bought! The key is the cooking and reduction part that makes it so good. A family keeper! We hope it will be for your family too."

2 tablespoons unsalted butter

1 cup finely chopped sweet onions

½ cup finely chopped celery

¼ cup finely chopped yellow sweet pepper

2 cloves garlic, finely chopped

2 (8-ounce) cans tomato sauce

¼ cup molasses

½ cup brown sugar

½ cup ketchup

1 tablespoon Worcestershire sauce

1½ teaspoons prepared yellow mustard

1 tablespoon apple cider vinegar

Dash of nutmeg and cinnamon

¼ teaspoon baking soda

¼ teaspoon smoked paprika (or more to taste)

¼ teaspoon hot sauce (or more to taste)

Salt and pepper, to taste

In a medium saucepan melt the butter over medium heat and add the onions, celery, peppers, and garlic. Cook gently until the onion is translucent.

Then add the remaining ingredients and bring to a boil.

Reduce the heat to low and simmer slowly for 30 to 45 minutes until the sauce has thickened some.

Add salt and pepper to taste and additional hot sauce and smoked paprika if you want!

Cool and ladle into sterilized jars with good lids. Store in the refrigerator or freeze for future use.

Quesadogas

SERVES 4. OH, WHO ARE WE KIDDING? SERVES 2.

All you will need for this wonderful and easy outdoor dinner is a cast iron skillet over a campfire, or your camp stove. We'd use the top of your cooler as a "table" for the preparations. And may we suggest some tequila? That was a long hike or ride, wasn't it?

1 cup shredded cheddar cheese

1 cup shredded Monterey Jack cheese

2 ripe avocados, pitted, peeled, and cut into pieces

1 tablespoon vegetable oil

4 hot dogs

8 flour tortillas

Chili powder, to taste

1 (15-ounce) can nacho cheese sauce, divided

1 cup Cowgirl Crude Salsa (see next page) or any salsa of your choice

Sour cream

Pre-measure the shredded cheeses into zip-top bags and cut up the avocados at home. (**Cowgirl tip:** Add a little lemon juice to the avocado bag to keep them green.) Pack the cheeses, avocado, salsa, hot dogs, and sour cream in a cooler until ready to cook.

Put the skillet over the fire on a grill and add the vegetable oil.

While the oil is heating, grill your hot dogs over the fire on a stick.

Top one tortilla with some of the cheddar, Monterey Jack, diced avocado, and chili powder. Cover the first tortilla with a second tortilla, and spread the top tortilla with some nacho cheese sauce and salsa. Place a hot dog at one end and roll up the tortillas around the hot dog. (Hint: You want to secure this roll with a toothpick.)

Put the Quesadoga in the skillet and cook until golden and crispy, about 3 to 4 minutes.

Serve with sour cream for dipping, as well as more nacho cheese sauce.

Cowgirl Crude Salsa

The following recipe was first published in The Cowgirl's Cookbook: Recipes for Your Home on the Range.

3 ripe tomatoes, chopped
¼–½ cup minced hot peppers (fresh
  or canned)
½ cup finely chopped onion
Tabasco or other hot sauce, to taste
Salt and pepper, to taste
¾ cup Spanish olives, chopped
  (optional)

Combine all the ingredients. Refrigerate at least 1 hour before serving.

Store in the refrigerator for up to 1 week.

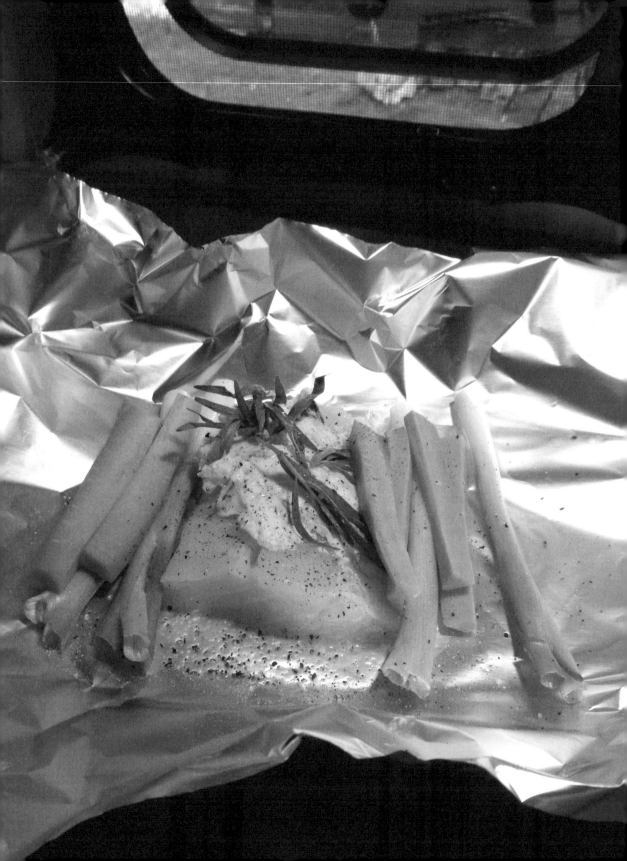

Seaside Fish Wrap for One

SERVES 1

A warm summer evening, the campfire is going nicely, your camp chair is set up, there is a cold beverage nearby, and you reach into your cooler and pull out a foil pack for dinner.

Who says you have to do a chicken breast? Try fish instead. It's a nice change.

You will want to use heavy-duty foil for your foil pack (or double wrap it with regular foil) so it won't break open when you are grilling it over the open fire. Prepare this packet at home and keep it cool in a cooler until dinner. Of course, you can make more than one, just double the recipe for two. Triple for three . . . and so on.

Nonstick cooking spray
1 fillet fish, your choice (we used halibut—firm and great flavor)
2 tablespoons butter
2 carrots, peeled and cut into sticks
2 green onions, cut to desired length
Salt and pepper, to taste

Spray your piece of foil with nonstick cooking spray.

Place the fish in the middle of the foil. Top with the butter, carrots, and green onions.

Season to taste with the salt and pepper. Fold up the sides of the foil. Then fold over the other sides to make a sealed foil pack.

Place on the grill over the campfire for about 30 minutes, depending on the thickness of the fish. Open the foil packet carefully because it got pretty hot in there!

Smokey Beans

SERVES 4

Good news! You can make this filling and hearty bean dish in your slow cooker at home. Then freeze it in coffee cans with good lids until you are ready to head out to camp. When the fire is going well, pour the defrosted beans into a Dutch oven or a cast iron skillet with a lid (or use aluminum foil) and heat it right over the fire while you grill a steak. Serve alongside a simple green salad.

1 pound lean ground beef
6 slices thick bacon, cut into ¼ -inch pieces
½ cup chopped sweet onion
1 (16-ounce) can baked beans
1 (16-ounce) can dark red kidney beans, drained
1 (8-ounce) can corn, drained
1 cup ketchup
½ cup brown sugar
2 teaspoons liquid smoke
2 tablespoons white vinegar
1 teaspoon salt
1 teaspoon pepper

Brown the ground beef and bacon in a skillet and drain off the fat.

Place all the ingredients into a 7-quart Crock-Pot and stir well.

Cover and cook on low setting for 5 hours (or high setting for 3 hours).

Alternatively, you can cook the beans over the campfire in your Dutch oven, making sure everything gets cooked well. If you're packing the ingredients for the campsite, we recommend keeping all the canned goods in the brown paper bag with handles from the store; mix the liquid smoke, brown sugar, vinegar, and ketchup together and store in an air-tight plastic container until ready to use; and keep the beef and bacon in the cooler.

HITTING THE ROAD IN AN RV

How do you go into the great outdoors to spend some time? Do you pack in on a horse? Perhaps you hike and backpack, or you simply load up a picnic in your car or truck and head to the beach or the mountains. Even a lovely park can help you escape into the outdoors, if only for a little while.

Some prefer to take their "home away from home" wherever they roam. We're talking about an RV—a recreational vehicle—with pretty much all the comforts of home: a bed instead of the hard ground; a small toilet that sure as heck beats the nightly trip with a flashlight. Most have air conditioning, as well as heat, and, best of all, cooking can be done inside without having to start a fire.

There are various types of RVs from self-driving ones that feature a full kitchen, to teardrop-style ones that are cute-as-a-bug little beds on wheels with a lift area for cooking, to mid-size RVs (both bumper pull, as well as self-driving). There's really something for everyone!

If you're looking to purchase an RV, be sure to consider what appliances and space the RV you are looking at has to prepare meals. A stovetop propane burner? A handy ice box stowed under the counter? Enough counter space to prepare veggies and fruit? Cupboards to hold everything you might need for a one-day, two-day, or longer trip? And last of all, a sink! The taps in RV sinks are pretty great in that most can either pull water directly from your freshwater tank using a pump, or allow water in from the outside tap. This makes for a versatile experience and allows for camping with or without hookups. Just remember, the water in a freshwater tank is limited, making it important to ration water during stints without water hookups.

We've put together some pretty wonderful recipes in this cookbook that are "road tested." If you are parked and set up in a camping spot for RVs, there are always fire pits and picnic tables, making your dining experience truly magical. Or, simply find a handy log. Unfold a few collapsible aluminum chairs, relax, and enjoy all that Mother Nature has provided.

Spider Corn Cake

SERVES 6

This is a revised recipe found in a very old cookbook of ours from New England. A long time ago, the old-fashioned term for an iron skillet was "spider"—a cast iron skillet with legs for baking in the fire. We know the recipe says "cake," but this is more like corn bread with a pancake texture than a dessert cake. It is served with maple syrup or honey and has a fascinating instruction that has you pouring "sweet milk" (which we substituted with heavy cream) that forms a thin layer of cream in the middle that makes it really moist. We love serving this for breakfast! It can be made ahead, stored in your cooler, and reheated easily.

¾ cup cornmeal
1 cup all-purpose flour
1 teaspoon baking powder
½ teaspoon baking soda
¾ teaspoon kosher salt
2 tablespoons butter, melted
2 cups buttermilk or sour milk (see note below)
½ cup sugar
2 eggs
1 teaspoon vanilla extract
1 cup heavy cream
Maple syrup or honey (for topping)

Preheat the oven to 350°F and arrange a rack in the middle of the oven. Grease a 10-inch cast iron skillet—your "spider"—with butter. (You can use any oven-safe skillet of the same size.)

Place the skillet in the oven to heat while you mix the batter.

Whisk together the cornmeal, flour, baking powder, baking soda, and salt in a bowl. Set aside.

In a larger bowl, whisk the melted butter, buttermilk (or sour milk), sugar, eggs, and vanilla until well combined.

Add the dry ingredients to the wet ingredients and stir until just combined and set aside to rest for a few minutes.

Remove the hot skillet from the oven and add the batter to the pan. At this point, pour the heavy cream into the center of the batter. (Yes, it really works and we were skeptical about this, too!)

Put the skillet back in the oven and bake for 40 to 50 minutes. Be sure to check it at 40 minutes. It should be golden brown and a little wobbly and soft in the middle. Take it out when it is done and let it rest to cool.

Serve warm with either maple syrup or honey.

Note on making sour milk: Whenever a recipe calls for buttermilk and you don't have it on hand, you can use sour milk to substitute. You can make sour milk by adding 1½ tablespoons apple cider vinegar or lemon juice to 2 cups of milk and letting this sit for 15 minutes before using.

Whiskey and Pineapple BBQ Sauce

MAKES ABOUT 3 CUPS

What do you get when you combine "Howdy" and "Aloha"? This simple-to-make and terrific barbecue sauce, that's what! We love anything at all with Pendleton Whisky in it, but any old whiskey or bourbon will do for this great sauce. Try this at your next grill party on ham steaks, chicken wings, pork chops, pork ribs, steak . . . you get the idea!

1½ cups brown sugar
1 cup ketchup
1 cup water
½ cup whiskey or bourbon
⅓ cup blackstrap molasses
½ teaspoon sea salt
½ teaspoon pepper
½ teaspoon garlic powder
½ teaspoon onion powder

Pour all the ingredients into a medium-size saucepan and bring it to a boil.

Reduce the heat and simmer for 30 to 40 minutes, until the sauce is thick and reduced by about half.

Use immediately, or store this in a sealed container in the refrigerator for up to a week.

Chapter 5

SOUPS AND SIDE DISHES

Credit: Gina Keesling

Bean Clutter

MAKES 10 (2-CUP) SERVINGS

Our friend Gina Keesling has, we think, three hands. One is running her business, Hoofprints, your source for unique horsey products; another is restoring and maintaining a historic old farmhouse; and yet another hand cares for her horses and other high-maintenance animals. She says, "This recipe is an adaptation of one that I saw in a magazine when my son was about half grown. With our busy schedule I don't often cook, so [I] try to find meal ideas that we can grab out of the fridge and eat without a lot of prep. After I'd made this the first time and realized it was so good and fairly healthy, I included some meat when I made it the second time. I find myself making giant bowls of it fairly often."

We think this is a great thing to take in your icebox in your RV, or in a cooler for a picnic. This recipe yields a lot of servings, but it freezes well so you can make it go a long, long way. This pairs wonderfully with cottage cheese, and there are all your food groups on one plate.

3 (15-ounce) cans black-eyed peas

1 (15-ounce) can garbanzo beans (chickpeas)

1 (15-ounce) can black beans

1 (15-ounce) can cannellini (white) beans

1 (15-ounce) can black olives, sliced in half

2 stalks celery, coarsely chopped

2 carrots, coarsely chopped

1 small/medium green pepper, seeded and coarsely chopped

1 small/medium red pepper, seeded and coarsely chopped

1 small/medium yellow pepper, seeded and coarsely chopped

4 cups shredded cabbage (you can cheat and buy coleslaw mix—we did)

3 green onions, thinly sliced

1 pound your choice of meat (optional—we like ham, smoked turkey, kielbasa, or spicy ground sausage)

For the dressing:

¾ cup red wine vinegar or apple cider vinegar

½ cup olive oil

2–3 tablespoons fresh dill (or to taste)

1 tablespoon ground cumin (or to taste)

1½ teaspoons sea salt

1 teaspoon pepper

Mix all the beans and vegetables together in a giant bowl.

Cook and chop the meat into bite-size pieces or slices. Add the meat to the bowl.

Mix the dressing ingredients in a smaller bowl, then drizzle over the bean-veggie-meat mixture. Toss to coat. Serve chilled.

Chanterelle Mushroom Soup

SERVES 6

In the fall, there is nothing more fun than hunting for mushrooms. We (caution, pay attention) ALWAYS take a mushroom guide with us to be sure we are not picking something that could kill us. Chanterelles are pretty easy to spot and even better to eat. We got about 5 pounds of these golden treasures. We came right home and made this delicate and simple soup, which we froze, for the first course for Thanksgiving dinner to remind us of that lovely day out in the woods.

2 tablespoons olive oil
1 sweet onion, finely chopped
3 cloves garlic, minced
2 cups chanterelle mushroom, carefully washed and roughly chopped
3 tablespoons all-purpose flour
2 cups vegetable stock
1 cup heavy cream or half-and-half
Salt and pepper, to taste

Heat the olive oil in your soup pot over medium-high heat. Then add the onions and sauté them until they are translucent. Add the garlic, cooking and stirring for 1 more minute.

Add the mushrooms into the pot. Cook them for about 6 minutes, or until they are soft and have released any of the liquid from cleaning.

Sprinkle the flour over the mushroom and onion mixture and stir to coat them well. Now whisk in the vegetable stock.

Bring this to a boil, reduce the heat to low, and simmer for about 5 minutes, stirring now and then. It will thicken.

Add the cream and the salt and pepper. Simmer for 10 more minutes, stirring now and then.

Serve immediately with a good French bread and butter as a first course, or as the best lunch you ever had.

Cold Melon Soup

SERVES 2 LARGE OR 4 SMALL SERVINGS

You are browsing the roadside fruit and vegetable stand when you spy a beautiful cantaloupe that is just perfect and ready to eat. Our father's favorite summer dessert was cantaloupe with lime sherbet. But maybe you are a bit bored with the usual sliced melon or half melon with a scoop of sherbet. Try this wonderful, refreshing cold summer soup. We like it served with leftover chicken or cold cuts and a simple green salad.

1 medium ripe cantaloupe, peeled, seeded, and diced (about 4 cups)

3 tablespoons lime juice

¼–½ teaspoon salt, to taste

Pinch of ground ginger (or more if you like ginger)

Mint sprigs (optional)

Put the diced melon in a blender (1 cup at a time) or food processor. Blend to puree and transfer to a bowl. Then add the lime juice, salt, and ginger and stir until well combined. Cover and chill for 2 hours or longer in the refrigerator until ready to serve. Garnish with sprigs of mint from your garden or the farm stand.

Corn Ensalada

SERVES 2

You might want to keep this recipe for another wonderful salad from Lorrie Turner a secret. It goes great with fish, but, really, this salad can be paired with everything from chicken to beef, or even to top a taco.

6 ears fresh corn, cut from the cob
2 tablespoons extra-virgin olive oil
1 green pepper, seeded and sliced
1 red pepper, seeded and sliced
2 small yellow squash, sliced
2 small zucchinis, sliced
½ cup chopped green onion
1 cup chopped cilantro

For the dressing:
6 tablespoons extra-virgin olive oil
¼ cup white wine vinegar
1½ teaspoons chili powder
2 cloves garlic, minced
1 teaspoon oregano
1 teaspoon cumin

Cut the corn off the cob and add it to a cast iron skillet. Add the 2 tablespoons of extra-virgin olive oil and cook over high heat just until the corn is lightly browned and has a smoky smell, about 4 minutes.

Transfer corn to a very large salad bowl and add the remaining salad ingredients.

Combine all the dressing ingredients in a jar with a lid, and shake until well-blended. Pour over the salad. Chill in the refrigerator and toss again before serving.

If you're taking this camping, transfer the salad to a large zip-top bag and store in a cooler at the campsite. This salad will last up to 5 days and seems to get better with age.

Fresh corn can be substituted with 2 cups of either canned or frozen corn.

Credit: Lorrie Turner

Daddy's Parsnips

SERVES 4

Our father was a man of simple tastes. He was a tugboat captain, as well as a friend of loggers all over the Pacific Northwest, and he liked his food simple.

He especially liked fried parsnips, and he would cook them for a Saturday lunch for himself. He would tell us they "tasted just like fried trout." Robin flatly refused to partake in them, but Jill was a dutiful daughter and she ate them. She was curious to re-create what Daddy thought was the "best vegetable ever." Surprisingly, they do taste a little bit like fried trout. But more importantly they really are quite good and simple to make.

6 large parsnips, washed, peeled, and
   cut lengthwise (snip off both ends)
1 stick (½ cup) butter
¼ cup all-purpose flour
½ teaspoon salt
½ teaspoon pepper

Put the peeled and cut parsnips in a saucepan with water to cover and bring to a boil. This "sweetens" them and makes them easier to fry. Boil on medium heat for about 10 minutes. Drain them, and dry them on a paper towel.

Melt the butter in a frying pan. In a shallow bowl, dredge the parsnip pieces in the flour and put in the sizzling butter.

Fry them, turning often, until light brown. Season with a little salt and pepper as they cook.

Note: Parsnips, peeled and chopped, are wonderful cooked with potatoes to mash and in a vegetable soup, too.

Delicata Squash—Two Ways

SERVES 4

Perusing the farm-fresh offerings at a roadside stand, we came upon a long, grooved, and striped green-and-yellow squash. We had never seen one like it before. "That's the sweetest squash you will ever eat," the farmer assured us. Well, OK, we'll try it. Jill is on her fifth or maybe her sixth delicata squash and she can assure you, it is the sweetest you will ever eat. Robin is not far behind. Here are two ways to enjoy this succulent squash side dish. You can eat them skin and all!

Cooking spray
1 delicata squash, washed, seeded, and cut length-wise in half
2 tablespoons vegetable oil
1 teaspoon cinnamon
1 teaspoon raw (Turbinado) sugar (you can also use brown)
½ teaspoon ground ginger

Preheat the oven to 425°F.

Spray a baking sheet with cooking spray.

Cut each squash half into ¼-inch "crescents."

In a small bowl, combine the oil, cinnamon, sugar, and ginger. Put the crescents in the bowl and stir to coat them evenly.

Place them on the baking sheet, making sure they are not touching one another. Bake for 10 minutes, then flip them and bake for another 10 minutes or until they are golden brown.

Our friend and cowgirl Kate Aspen suggested another way to enjoy this sweet squash, too.

Cooking spray
1 delicata squash, washed, seeded, and cut length-wise in half
Salt and pepper, to taste

Preheat the oven to 425°F.

Spray a baking sheet with cooking spray.

Place the halved squash face down on the sheet—one squash for two people.

Bake for 10 minutes, then turn them over and season with salt and pepper. Bake for another 10 minutes or until fork tender.

Kate serves these cold with cottage cheese in the middle and topped with halved cherry tomatoes. She also sprinkles them with cinnamon sugar.

Fiddlehead Ferns

SERVES 4-6

Fiddleheads are a true early spring vegetable and not found in the desert. Deep wooded areas of the East and West Coasts are where you will find these tightly coiled fern "babies" that will eventually grow into tall ferns. Fiddleheads have a grassy, springlike flavor with a hint of nuttiness. Many people agree that they taste like a cross between asparagus and young spinach. Some detect an artichoke flavor as well, and even a bit of mushroom. Worth the hunt!

1 pound fiddleheads, rinsed well
1 tablespoon butter
Salt and pepper, to taste

Boil or steam the fiddleheads for 5 to 10 minutes, or until tender. Drain.

Jill likes these with just butter, salt, and pepper to taste.

Credit: © Getty Images

Gina's Some Like It Hot Cauliflower

SERVES 4-6

This is not your mother's cauliflower, trust us. Gina Keesling developed this amazing, fast, easy, delicious (and healthy) recipe using the hot sauce she sells on her website. She says, "I have fixed this with the lid on the dish, and the lid off. It seems to cook a bit faster with the lid on, and it's a little moister. You can add a small amount of water, too; the resulting steam seems to speed up the cooking process."

1 large head cauliflower

2 tablespoons olive oil

2 tablespoons Farriers' Fitting Hot Sauce (or any hot sauce, but you'll find the link to buy this amazing sauce in the Sources at the back of this book)

1 tablespoon paprika

½ teaspoon salt

¼ teaspoon pepper

Preheat the oven to 375°F.

Carefully cut the green leaves off the bottom of the cauliflower, removing the woody stem, but leaving the head intact. Rinse, pat dry, and set aside.

Add the oil, hot sauce, paprika, salt, and pepper into a small bowl, using a fork to mix it all together.

Put the cauliflower into a large zip-top bag, making sure it fits and you can zip the top. Now pour the wet ingredients into the bag with the cauliflower. Close the bag and swish it around a bit to mix up the ingredients, making sure the cauliflower is coated all over. Press out the air and seal the bag completely. You can put this in the refrigerator for as long as you want if you aren't cooking it right away.

When you are ready to bake it, open the bag and place the cauliflower, cut (or stem) side down into a greased baking dish (we used Pam). Drizzle the remaining sauce over the top of the cauliflower.

Bake for about 60 minutes. This time will vary according to the size of the cauliflower. Check with a fork, starting at about 45 minutes, and remove from the oven when it's tender all the way through.

Cut into wedges and serve, spooning a little of the remaining sauce in the cooking pan over the wedges.

Gretchen's Salad

MAKES ABOUT 4 CUPS

Jill's friend Gretchen Wilson rode with her all over the place for over twenty years. They went to horse shows together, happily competing against one another. They would go to the Oregon Coast and ride the dunes and sandy beaches. They horse camped and rode Mt. Hood and the Barlow Trail. Gretchen was as nuts about horses as Jill. This is what Gretchen always brought for the salad when they camped, along with two great steaks from her farm-raised beef, cooked over the campfire grill. Jill thinks of her friend whenever she makes it.

1 head fresh broccoli, washed, torn, and trimmed into florets

1 cup shredded cheddar cheese

½ cup salted sunflower seeds

¼ cup rice vinegar

Mix the ingredients together in a large bowl and keep in the refrigerator. This salad won't spoil, it is very good for you, and it has just the right amount of tartness.

Hobo Stew

SERVES 4 RAVENOUS CAMPERS

Jill was a Brownie and then a Girl Scout. Her fearless troop leader took the little girls down to the shores of Puget Sound one Saturday to make this Hobo Stew for lunch. It was freezing cold, the fires they had to make wouldn't start, and Jill remembers she was miserable kneeling on the small rocks that made up the shoreline. Years later, she re-created this old standby so you can enjoy a hot stew when you get back from your hike or ride. You can cook this in a slow cooker (option #1) if you have an RV and an electrical outlet, or you can cook this in the iron Dutch oven over the campfire from breakfast (option #2). The ingredients stay the same for both.

Cooking spray (slow cooker) or 2 tablespoons cooking oil (Dutch oven)
1 pound lean ground beef
1½ cups chopped onion
Salt and pepper
2 cups peeled and cubed potatoes
1 (16-ounce) package frozen mixed vegetables
1 (14.5-ounce) can diced tomatoes
1 (8-ounce) can tomato sauce
2 cups beef broth
2 cups water

Option 1: For the slow cooker

Grease the slow cooker with cooking spray.

Cook the beef and onions in a large nonstick skillet. Season with the salt and pepper, and cook for 5 to 7 minutes until beef is cooked through and onions are tender. Drain off any excess fat.

Add the ground beef and onions to the slow cooker along with the potatoes, mixed vegetables, diced tomatoes, tomato sauce, broth, and water.

Cover and cook on low for 6 to 8 hours until potatoes are tender.

Option 2: For the campfire Dutch oven

Start the fire until there are good, hot coals. Place the Dutch oven over the coals on a grill.

Put 2 tablespoons of bacon fat (saved from breakfast) or vegetable oil in the bottom of the Dutch oven and add the beef and onions. Season with salt and pepper and cook for 5 to 7 minutes until beef is cooked through and onions are tender.

Add all the other ingredients (don't drain the cans). Mix everything together.

Put the lid on the Dutch oven and cook until the potatoes are done (about 10 minutes), stirring now and then.

Mashed Turnips and Potatoes

SERVES 4

Both of these root vegetables store quite nicely over the winter. You will come to love this side dish that has its beginning in Ireland. We love it and it's on our Thanksgiving table each year now.

2 turnips, peeled and cubed (place them in cold water with a little salt to keep them from browning)
6 medium potatoes, peeled and cubed
2 tablespoons olive oil
1 tablespoon salt (or to taste)
1 tablespoon pepper (or to taste)
½ cup whole milk, warmed
2 tablespoons butter, melted
1 tablespoon crushed thyme

Preheat the oven to 400°F.

Rinse and dry the turnips and potatoes and place them on a baking sheet in a single layer. Drizzle them with olive oil and sprinkle with the salt and pepper.

Roast the vegetables for 20 minutes.

Remove the pan from the oven, stir them around, and continue roasting for 20 minutes longer. The potatoes and turnips will be tender and lightly golden brown.

Put the potatoes and turnips into a bowl and mash well with a potato masher. You can also use your stand mixer or a handheld mixer. Add the milk, butter, and thyme and mix well. Still have a few lumps? That's fine!

GRIT AND SAND: PIONEER COWGIRL AND PHOTOGRAPHER EVELYN CAMERON

Cowgirls have a saying for a person who can stand up and do the job, no matter what the circumstances. That person has "grit and sand," and Evelyn Cameron certainly had it in spades while remaining a lady.

Terry, Montana, in Eastern Montana suited Evelyn Jephson Flower Cameron just fine when she and her husband, Ewen, arrived in 1889 from England. They had planned to raise and import polo ponies, but this

Janet Williams and Evelyn Cameron in Mrs. Cameron's garden holding turnips or beets. Saddled horse in background.

Credit: PAc 90-87.NB039H, Montana Historical Society Research Center Photograph Archives, Helena, MT

venture soon failed. They took in boarders on their ranch and it was there that Evelyn discovered her passion—photography. She photographed everything she saw, from cowboys to wolves, using a heavy camera with glass plates. She was always in a long split skirt, never wore a hat, and was sunburned to the color of tanned leather. She rode miles alone across the prairie to find her subjects.

To learn more about cowgirl photographer Evelyn Cameron and to see many of her photographs, visit evelyncameron.org. We urge you to look her up and see all the wonderful images she captured for us under amazing circumstances.

Group photo, picnic at Cross S Ranch with Evelyn Cameron behind table (hands clasped), August 28, 1921; group of people under cottonwood trees standing around picnic table with food covered with netting, Eastern Montana.

Credit: PAc 90-87.G036-002, Montana Historical Society Research Center Photograph Archives, Helena, MT

Native Trout Dip

1½ CUPS

The Salish women in this photo are smoking their trout over an open fire to keep through the winter. You can enjoy the taste of smoked trout with this very easy dip. You don't even have to go wading onto a cold river. Thanks to our mother for this handwritten recipe.

1 (8-ounce) tin smoked trout
1 cup cream cheese, softened
½ cup sour cream
1 small green onion, finely chopped
1 tablespoon Worcestershire sauce
1 teaspoon garlic powder
½ teaspoon lemon juice
Pepper, to taste

Mix all the ingredients in a bowl (or a storage container if you are RVing) and stir until well-blended. We like this on crackers before dinner, but you can also put a dollop on a beefsteak tomato slice on a bed of lettuce for a terrific salad. Cover leftovers tightly and refrigerate.

Credit: 954-715, Montana Historical Society Research Center Photograph Archives, Helena, MT

Old-Fashioned Coleslaw Dressing

1 CUP

This comes from our cowgirl friend in Kansas, Peggy Deal. This was her Granny's recipe and she treasures the yellowed and stained 3 x 5-inch index card her Granny wrote it on. Pour this dressing over chopped green cabbage, red cabbage, and a few shredded carrots, and you have a wonderful coleslaw salad as a side to a grilled something or sandwiches.

1 egg yolk
3 tablespoons sugar
1 tablespoon prepared mustard
2 tablespoons butter
½ cup white vinegar
½ cup half-and-half

In a medium saucepan, stir together the egg yolk, sugar, mustard, butter, and vinegar.

Whisk together over medium heat and boil until thick.

Remove from heat and let cool.

Whisk in the half-and-half.

Refrigerate in a clean glass jar with a lid until ready to use.

Remembrance Carrots

SERVES 4

Remember when you were little and your mother, as ours did, implored you to "eat your carrots"? That she told you it would be good for your eyes? Turns out our mothers were right. But when boiled until they were soft, we thought carrots were completely unappetizing, and we also felt that carrots were for horses. Period. Well! That went on for quite a few years until we discovered that there are many types of carrots, and the cutest of all are the little colored ones. Not only are they pretty to look at, they taste nothing at all like the carrots of our childhood. We hope you try them out.

12 garden-fresh carrots (no need to peel)
2 tablespoons brown sugar
3 tablespoons water
3 tablespoons olive oil
2 tablespoons fresh rosemary leaves, crushed
Salt and pepper, to taste

Preheat the oven to 375°F.

In a large bowl, combine all the ingredients.

Place the well-coated carrots into an 8 x 8-inch baking dish.

Bake uncovered for about 40 to 50 minutes, stirring now and then.

Watermelon and Tomato Summer Salad

SERVES 4

We could eat this all day long in the summer. We pine for it in the winter.

This salad travels well to a picnic in a cooler and is the perfect "What can I bring?" item for a summer barbecue potluck.

8 cups chopped seedless watermelon, cut into 1¼-inch chunks

3 cups chopped ripe heirloom tomatoes, cut into 1¼-inch chunks

1 teaspoon (or more) sea salt or coarse kosher salt

5 tablespoons extra-virgin olive oil, divided

3 tablespoons chopped fresh dill

3 tablespoons chopped fresh basil

3 tablespoons chopped fresh rosemary

Pepper, to taste

1 cup crumbed feta cheese

½ cup black kalamata olives, pitted

2 cups salad greens (optional—we like a spinach/arugula blend)

Combine watermelon and tomatoes in a large bowl.

Sprinkle with the salt and toss to mix; let this stand for 15 minutes.

Add 4 tablespoons of the oil and the herbs to the melon-tomato mixture. Season to taste with pepper and more salt, if desired. Add the feta cheese and olives to the bowl, then stir gently to combine.

Optional: Add your favorite salad greens to the bowl with the remaining 1 tablespoon of oil, and toss the ingredients until everything is well-coated.

Chapter 6
COWGIRL DESSERTS AND DRINKS

Browned Butter Blueberry Skillet

SERVES 8

Your cast iron skillet is perfect for this wonderful dessert—or perhaps breakfast? This recipe came from a woman who had a u-pick blueberry farm we loved to go to and pick buckets and buckets of the sweet indigo-blue berries. The beauty of the browned butter is that it also seasons your skillet. Fresh or frozen (if it's the dead of winter), this is a wonderful thing to do with these delightful little blue gems.

1 stick (½ cup) butter

4 ounces (½ stick) cream cheese, room temperature

¾ cup plus 2 tablespoons sugar

1 teaspoon vanilla extract

1 cup all-purpose flour

2 teaspoons baking powder

Pinch of salt

1 cup whole milk

2 cups frozen tiny blueberries, thawed (or 3 cups of fresh blueberries, washed)

Preheat your oven to 350°F.

Put the butter in the skillet (you can use a medium-size baking dish) and bake in the oven until the butter is slightly browned and bubbling, about 8 to 10 minutes.

In a small bowl, combine the softened cream cheese, 2 table-spoons of the sugar, and the vanilla. Stir this until it is well-blended. Set aside.

In a large bowl, sift the flour, baking powder, and salt together. Stir in the milk and the remaining ¾ cup of sugar.

Take the skillet out of the oven and immediately pour the browned butter into the batter. Stir it up until you can no longer see the melted butter.

Pour the batter back into the hot skillet or baking dish. Scatter the blueberries evenly over the top, then dot the cream cheese mixture all around.

Bake for 1 hour or until brown.

Let it cool on a wire rack until it's warm and serve with vanilla ice cream.

Dandy Dandelion Wine

MAKES 1 GALLON

Please, don't spray these as weeds! Welcome them to your garden or search for them in the fields because they are packed with vitamin C, vitamin B6, thiamine, riboflavin, calcium, iron, potassium, manganese, folate, magnesium, copper, phosphorus, vitamin K, and vitamin A. The leaves are wonderful in smoothies and salads, and the flowers brighten a salad. Want to try dandelion wine? Here's how!

1 gallon fresh-picked, open dandelion blossoms (it's very important that the flowers have not been sprayed with weed killer)

3 pounds (6 ¾ cups) sugar

3 or 4 lemons, juice, skin, seeds, etc., cut into chunks, chopped

3 or 4 oranges, juice, skin, seeds, etc., cut into chunks, chopped

2 packages wine yeast

Rinse the flowers well and put them in a 2-gallon (or larger) open crock and pour boiling water over them until they are just covered.

Cover the crock with cheesecloth and let it sit at room temperature for 3 days. Then, using the cheesecloth as your strainer, squeeze all the juice out of the flowers. Throw those flowers away, but save the liquid.

Put the liquid into a big pot and add the sugar, lemons, and oranges. Boil this mixture for 30 minutes with the top on the pot.

Remove this from the heat and let cool to lukewarm. Pour this into the crock and add the yeast.

Re-cover with that cheesecloth and let this concoction brew for 2 or 3 weeks in a cool and dark place. Check on it now and then; it ought to be bubbling or fizzy on the top. When the bubbles have stopped and all is quiet in the crock, it's ready!

Filter through more cheesecloth to strain out the fruit chunks. Ladle into pint jars and screw the lids on tightly.

This wine packs a punch. Don't say we didn't warn you!

Credit: Shutterstock

Happy Cake

1 TWO-LAYER CAKE

This old-time recipe dates from the Great Depression when ingredients were scarce because of the money they cost, so a treat like a cake was very rare. This cake is easy to make and it keeps very well. It's perfect to take along for a potluck picnic.

3 cups all-purpose flour

2 cups sugar

1 teaspoon salt

6 tablespoons cocoa powder

2 teaspoons baking soda

½ teaspoon ground ginger

¾ cup melted coconut oil (at room temperature)

2 teaspoons vanilla extract

2 cups lukewarm water

1 tablespoon strong black coffee, cold

2 tablespoons apple cider vinegar

Jam or jelly (for filling)

Powdered sugar (for dusting)

Preheat your oven to 375°F.

Grease and flour two 9-inch cake pans.

Combine the flour, sugar, salt, cocoa powder, baking soda, and ginger in a bowl and whisk together.

Add the coconut oil, vanilla, and water and mix well. Add the coffee and the apple cider vinegar, stirring to break up any lumps.

Pour the batter into the prepared cake pans and bake for 25 minutes.

Allow cakes to cool on a rack before spreading the jam between the layers. Stack the cakes and dust with powdered sugar.

Note: We filled the two layers with raspberry jam, but any jam would do nicely!

Hood River Bing Cherry Shrub

MAKES 3 CUPS

Our grandmother, Marguerite Millikin Peters, belonged to a ladies' book club in Hood River, Oregon, in the 1930s. The ladies of Hood River liked coming to Marguerite's when it was her turn to entertain the monthly gathering to enjoy Marguerite's Bing Cherry Shrub that she made herself and served in a crystal decanter with small, elegant cordial glasses. We are certain the ladies knew the shrub was alcoholic, but, because it was quite genteel and elegant, that made it alright to have two or three (or possibly more) small glasses while they discussed the newest book, which was quite possibly Gone with the Wind.

The early English version of the shrub arose from the medicinal cordials of the fifteenth century and later became a popular way to combine alcohol with fruits. You can double or triple this recipe depending on how much you will be using.

1 cup Bing cherries, pitted and lightly crushed
1 cup sugar
1 cup apple cider vinegar or red wine

Combine the fruit and sugar in a large bowl. Refrigerate this for several days, stirring at least once a day. The sugar will draw out the liquid from the fruit, and when it's ready it will look like fruit floating around in a thick syrup. Taste it to make certain you have the essence of the fruit you have chosen.

Strain out the fruit with a wire mesh strainer. Save the sugared fruit in a separate container. It makes a great addition to plain yogurt or oatmeal, or can be eaten straight for a dessert with cream or as a topping for ice cream.

Then add your vinegar or wine to the fruit syrup and stir.

Bottle your shrub and wait a few days before serving so the fruit syrup and the vinegar or wine have "married." Keep it refrigerated until ready to use.

Pour 2 or 3 tablespoons (Marguerite used a sterling soup spoon) into each cordial glass and top with a spurt of club soda. This really was an early-day spritzer! Champagne would also be a very special addition. We like it with a small dash of vodka, as well as soda water.

The shrub ought to remain fresh for several months, but if you start to see bubbles, or it becomes "slimy," it is turning bad and is no longer useable.

Cowgirl tip: You can make a shrub with any kind of fruit and wine/vinegar combination. Just make sure to pair your fruit with the right wine. For instance, white wine with apples, peaches, pears, or Queen Anne cherries. Red wine with Bing cherries, and all other berries. Any other fruit-based vinegars can be used, but do not use white vinegar as it is too strong.

Lovely Lavender Tea

SERVES 2

Who doesn't like lavender? Its sweet, floral flavor with lemon and citrus notes makes a perfect cowgirl tea, soothing after a hard day.

1 cup (8 ounces) spring or filtered water

2 tablespoons fresh lavender buds or dried lavender flowers

Bring the water to a rolling boil in a large saucepan.

Place the lavender flowers in a tea infuser basket or tea pincer and place it in a tea cup.

Pour the boiling water into the cup. Steep the lavender flowers in the hot water for 8 to 10 minutes. The longer you steep, the stronger the flavor will become.

Remove the tea infuser or strain the loose flowers using a fine mesh strainer. You can drink it as is, or we like to add some honey, sugar, or lemon.

Credit: Shutterstock

Miss Dorothy's Whiskey Pound Cake

MAKES 2 LOAVES

When we were thinking about the recipes that would be good for cowgirls to make and enjoy for this book it occurred to me that an old-fashioned pound cake would be the perfect "cake" to make and take on all sorts of adventures. For one thing, pound cake is nearly indestructible. It's sturdy! It's delicious plain, toasted over the campfire, or covered in fresh berries with a little sugar mixed in for a wonderful dessert at the end of the day.

We reached out to an old friend, Dorothy Johnson, who camps a great deal, usually by herself with only her Australian Shepherd and her 18-year-old gelding who is, she says, "unflappable." Here is what she sent me, and true to Miss Dorothy's outlook on life, it contains a little surprise—one we are enthusiastically promoting here.

2 sticks (½ pound) unsalted butter

½ cup vegetable shortening

3 cups sugar

1 teaspoon vanilla extract

1 cup whole milk

5 eggs

¼ cup whiskey (optional! Should you choose not to add the whiskey, increase the milk to 1¼ cups.)

3 cups all-purpose flour

½ teaspoon baking powder

¼ teaspoon salt

Preheat the oven to 325°F.

Grease and flour two 9 x 5-inch loaf pans.

Cream together the butter, shortening, sugar, vanilla, and milk. Add the eggs, one at a time, and continue beating and creaming with each one. Add the whiskey to this creamed mix and stir.

Sift together the flour, baking powder, and salt in a separate bowl, and add it to the creamed mixture, a little at a time, stirring well.

Pour the batter into the loaf pans and smooth the tops.

Bake for 1 hour and maybe 10 minutes more until the tops have "split" and they are nicely browned.

When cool, slice the cake to carry in your saddlebags, backpack, or cooler, well-wrapped in plastic wrap and then aluminum foil.

Cowgirl tip: You can make delicious trail sandwiches out of pound cake—our personal preference is butter and raspberry jam.

No Apples Pie

MAKES 1 PIE

This recipe is an old standard from the Depression era. It tastes and looks very much like an apple pie and certainly looks like the real deal, but it isn't. We won't tell if you don't! Whoever thought of it was a genius. There are many versions but this one is our favorite. This pie would travel very well (we would cut it into pieces and wrap those pieces in foil) and we'd also have wedges of cheddar cheese to go along with it.

2 teaspoons cream of tartar

2 cups sugar

1 ¾ cups water

2½ tablespoons lemon juice

1½ teaspoons vanilla extract

¾ teaspoon cinnamon (or more if you like)

¼ teaspoon nutmeg

2 pre-made pie crusts (you can buy these at the grocery store or make them if you are talented and/or not short of time)

48–50 classic butter crackers (such as Ritz or Late July), broken in half by hand

Preheat the oven to 425°F.

In a saucepan, whisk the cream of tartar into the sugar and then add the water, lemon juice, vanilla extract, cinnamon and nutmeg. Stir until dissolved. Bring the mixture to a boil over high heat and then reduce the heat to medium and simmer 20 to 30 minutes uncovered. You are looking for the sauce to reduce so it looks more like syrup, but it will still be pretty thin. Put it aside to cool some.

While the sauce is reducing, place one pre-made pie crust in a 9-inch pie pan and layer the broken crackers evenly on the bottom. Cut the second pie crust into lattice strips and set aside.

Gently spoon the sauce evenly over the crackers and place the lattice strips on top in a crisscross pattern. Seal the edges and flute as you like.

Place the pie in the oven and bake for 30 minutes or until the pie is golden brown.

For a picnic, serve with cheese, Cool Whip, whipped cream, or vanilla ice cream that can be kept cold in your cooler.

Peach Beach Cobbler

SERVES 4

A favorite spot on the Columbia River to RV or tent camp is Maryhill State Park, which is about 20 miles east of The Dalles, and over the Columbia River on the Washington side. It is immediately adjacent to Peach Beach. The area is known for their wonderful peaches grown in that warm sun by the river. It is Robin's tradition to go when the peaches are ripe and make peach jam and also prepare peach cobbler. Here is the recipe done on-site with an Omnia Oven (see Sources for this amazing invention), but this works just as well in a baking dish.

4 large, ripe peaches, peeled* and sliced
1 tablespoon brandy (optional, but oh so good!)
1 cup sugar, divided
1 cup all-purpose flour
1½ teaspoons baking powder
1 teaspoon salt
1 stick (½ cup) butter, softened
½ cup half-and-half
1 teaspoon vanilla extract

Prepare your Omnia Oven with a silicon liner with butter, or butter an 8 x 8-inch baking dish.

Combine the peaches, brandy, and ½ cup sugar in a medium pot and cook on medium for 5 minutes. Using a slotted spoon, remove the peaches and set aside.

Over medium-high heat reduce the juice left by the peaches to about half and set this aside separately from the peaches.

Whisk together the flour, the remaining ½ cup sugar, baking powder, and salt. Add the softened butter and mix well and then add the half-and-half and vanilla.

In either the Omnia Oven dish or a baking dish, put down about half of the peaches, then spread the batter over the peaches. Repeat this step with another layer of peaches and then the remainder of the batter. Pour on the reduced peach juices and sprinkle with sugar.

In the Omnia Oven, preheat the ring base of the Omnia for about 3 minutes on high. Place the pan with the peach mixture on the base and continue to cook on high for 6 minutes and then reduce the heat to medium-low and cook for about 30 to 40 minutes until done.

In a regular oven, preheat the oven to 350°F and bake in the middle of the oven for about 45 minutes or until done.

***Cowgirl tip:** Drop the peaches one by one into a pot of boiling water. Let them sit in this bath for 2 to 3 minutes. When you remove them, the furry peel slips right off.

Pumpkin Cutie Pies

SERVES 6

If these are not the cutest things you have ever made for Thanksgiving or a fall supper, then we give up. Robin came up with this brilliant way to make pumpkin pies without that dreary crust. Prepare for compliments!

6 baby or mini pumpkins (single serving size)
1 (30-ounce) can pumpkin pie mix
1 (5-ounce) can evaporated milk
2 eggs, lightly beaten

Preheat the oven to 350°F.

Prepare the little pumpkins by cutting about 1 inch around the stem and lifting off the tops. Scoop out the insides completely. (Really the same process as if you were going to carve them for Halloween, only you are making little baking cups instead.)

Place the hollowed out pumpkin shells on a baking sheet and bake them in the oven for 20 to 30 minutes.

While the pumpkins bake, make the filling by combining all the other ingredients in a bowl and mixing well.

Fill each partially baked pumpkin with about ½ to ⅔ cup of pumpkin pie filling. The filling should reach the rim but not go over it.

Bake until the filling is set, about 30 to 35 minutes.

Serve warm with a spoonful of whipped cream and garnish with a little cinnamon sugar.

Old-Fashioned Rhubarb Crisp

SERVES 4

In the spring, don't overlook rhubarb at the farmers' market or in your grocery store. You really ought to plant one if you have the space. They reward you year after year with bright red stalks. We were lucky enough as girls to have several rhubarb plants in our parents' garden, so it was always there for a pie or a crisp. Not only does it taste great, it's awfully good for you! A great source of antioxidants, vitamin K, and fiber, and what's not to like about that? This is a real treat straight from our childhood!

For the filling:

6 cups chopped fresh rhubarb, peeled and cut into 1-inch pieces
¼ cup all-purpose flour (or whole wheat, if you prefer)
¾ cup sugar
1 teaspoon lemon juice or zest

For the topping:

½ cup old-fashioned oats
½ cup all-purpose flour
½ cup brown sugar
6 tablespoons salted butter, cut into small cubes or bits

Preheat the oven to 375°F.

Lightly grease an 8 x 8-inch glass baking dish.

Mix the filling ingredients (rhubarb, flour, sugar, and lemon juice or zest) in a bowl and set aside.

Put the oats, flour, and brown sugar in another bowl and mix until combined. Add small bits of the butter into the dry mixture and pinch with your fingers (or cut it in) until the mixture is combined and crumbly.

Pour the filling mixture into your baking dish and spread it evenly. Then sprinkle the topping over it until well dispersed.

Put this in the oven and bake on the middle rack for 30 to 40 minutes until the top is golden and the rhubarb is bubbling up.

Enjoy with vanilla ice cream, thick cream, or whipped cream.

On the Road Brownies

SERVES 2

This delicious, RV-friendly dessert is baked in—what else?—the Omnia Oven*!

5 tablespoons plus 1 teaspoon butter
4 ounces dark chocolate (or 8
    tablespoons chocolate chips)
1 teaspoon vanilla extract
¾ cup sugar
1 teaspoon baking powder
Can of butter-flavored cooking spray
2 eggs

Melt the butter and the chocolate in a saucepan over medium heat, or you can melt it directly in the Omnia pan. Then add the vanilla, sugar, and baking powder. Stir to a smooth batter.

Add one egg at a time and stir until smooth.

Pour the batter into the silicone mold (if you don't have one, grease and flour the pan first).

Bake at low heat on your burner for about 20 minutes.

Test with a toothpick for doneness. There should be no wet batter left on the toothpick.

*This nifty, little device comes with full instructions and you can find more tasty recipes on their website.

Rhubarb and Strawberry Spring Pot Pies

MAKES 4 INDIVIDUAL POT PIES, OR 1 (2-QUART) CASSEROLE

FINALLY! Spring has sprung. Leaves are budding, daffodils are up, and we are ready for spring's bounty and that always includes rhubarb. It's a tonic after a long, cold winter. Strawberries are also in the store, so we put the two together and came up with these adorable one-serving desserts. You can substitute 6 cups of fresh blueberries, blackberries, or raspberries when they come into season, but for now, we are celebrating spring!

A note: Coauthor Robin Betty Johnson stitched the beautiful kitchen towel for Jill's spring birthday! Isn't it perfect?

For the filling:
4 cups sliced rhubarb
2 cups sliced strawberries
½ cup sugar
1 tablespoon cornstarch
1 teaspoon almond extract

For the pastry:
2 tablespoons sugar
1 cup all-purpose flour
1½ tablespoons baking powder
Pinch of salt
½ teaspoon cinnamon (optional)
½ stick (4 tablespoons) cold butter
1 egg, lightly beaten
½ teaspoon vanilla extract
¼ cup whole milk

Mix the filling ingredients together in a medium bowl. Then let it rest for about a half hour so the fruit absorbs all the sugar, cornstarch, and almond extract.

While the fruit is resting, preheat your oven to 350°F.

Lightly grease your little pie dishes or your large casserole dish with cooking spray.

In another bowl and using a fork or a whisk, combine the dry pastry ingredients (sugar through cinnamon).

Use a pastry blender or your hands (our preferred method) to cut in the butter. Mix together until it looks like crumbs and the butter is evenly distributed.

Now stir the wet ingredients (egg, vanilla, and milk) into this mixture. Spoon the fruit into the pie dishes or casserole dish.

Then, using another spoon, drop the "wet" topping onto the fruit, spreading it a bit toward the sides. (This is not a pastry crust it is more like a cobbler.)

Sprinkle raw Turbinado sugar on top for a glistening look. Regular sugar will work, too, but it won't look as "fancy."

Bake for 30 to 35 minutes until the crust is golden and the rhubarb/strawberry filling is bubbling. These would be awfully good with a dollop of whipped cream, vanilla bean ice cream, or a jug of heavy cream passed around to pour over your very own pie.

Sweet Apple Pie Moonshine

MAKES 8 CUPS (½ GALLON)

We hope you are safely parked. No plans of driving anywhere, or even going for a moonlight ride. Why? Because this adult beverage is the best relaxer after a hard day's drive or ride. Settle down, relax, and sip. Sleep tight!

4 cups apple juice
4 cups unfiltered apple cider
1½ cups sugar
4 cinnamon sticks
1½ cups caramel vodka

Bring the juice, cider, sugar, and cinnamon to a boil in a large saucepan. Cover and simmer for 1 hour.

Remove from the heat and let cool.

When it has cooled, pour in the flavored vodka.

Ladle this beverage into individual 8-ounce Mason jars with lids and store in a cool place.

Cowgirl tip: You can alter this recipe to suit your own personal tastes. Use less vodka, for instance. Or swap out the apple juice for peach, lemon, or cherry juice for a summer treat.

White Clover Tea

MAKES 4 CUPS

Believe us when we tell you that white clover blossoms make a wonderful, refreshing iced tea that is also highly nutritious. Why? Because the clover blossoms are high in vitamins and minerals. Feel free to add in a few fresh mint or lemon balm leaves to make it extra delicious.

This is the perfect wild foraged summer drink. Just make sure the clover blossoms are organic—no pesticide spray has been applied.

1 cup fresh white clover blossoms (or ½ cup dried blossoms), washed well in cold water
4 cups water
Honey, to taste
Lemon wedge
Mint leaves (optional)

Put the clover blossoms into a quart jar.

Boil the water, then pour it over the blossoms.

Let them steep for at least 30 minutes, then strain out the clover blossoms with a fine mesh strainer.

Stir in some honey while it is still warm.

Refrigerate.

Serve cold over ice with a lemon slice and a few mint leaves if you like.

Cowgirl tip: For a very special treat, enjoy this tea with the Lilac Jelly (page 151) spread over plain crackers. You will be delighted at what Mother Nature provides us with—for free!

Wild Ice Cream

SERVES 2

Does it get any wilder than snow ice cream? We think not! It did not snow often in Edmonds, Washington, but when it did—hooray! Gather up your ingredients, have your snow boots on, and here you go!

1 cup milk (any kind will do; our mother used evaporated milk)
½ cup sugar
1 teaspoon vanilla extract (optional)
Pinch of salt
7 or 8 cups *fresh* snow

In a large bowl (you will see why in a bit) whisk the ingredients until well mixed together.

Now, wearing your snow boots, rush outside and scoop up the snow.

Immediately fold the snow gently into the bowl until it has the texture of ice cream. This melts pretty fast, so have your serving bowls and spoons at the ready.

Of course, you can top this with any ice cream topping, but we liked it just simple, cold, and pure.

Chapter 7

PRESERVING AND PICKLING NATURE'S BOUNTY

Apple Pumpkin Butter

ABOUT 4 CUPS, DEPENDING ON DESIRED REDUCTION

Pumpkins are not just for jack-o'-lanterns. This is a wonderful way to celebrate fall produce, and it will make your house smell divine! Spread this on biscuits, toast, pancakes, or serve it with a pork roast.

3 cups unsweetened applesauce
   (canned or homemade)
1½ cups pumpkin puree (canned or
   homemade)
¾ cups packed brown sugar
3 tablespoons maple syrup
1 teaspoon pumpkin pie spice
1 teaspoon lemon juice

In a medium saucepan, add the applesauce and pumpkin puree and mix well.

Bring this mixture to a boil with the lid off, and then reduce the heat to low and simmer this mixture for an hour, mixing frequently.

To this partially reduced mixture, add the rest of the ingredients and bring to a boil again. Then reduce heat to low and let this mixture gently simmer, stirring often, for another 45 minutes until the butter is the consistency you desire.

Store in the refrigerator for a week or freeze.

PRESERVING AND PICKLING
AS A PASTIME

This image shows the 4-H club of Montrose, Colorado, circa 1936, proudly showing off their skills at filling Mason jars with all sorts of preserves to see their families though the winter. See the ribbons they won for their jarred fruits and vegetables? The teachers look very proud, and you will be too when you try some of our suggestions for keeping the flavors of summer all year round.

Apricot Jam

MAKES ABOUT 2 CUPS OR 4 (8-OUNCE) JARS

We don't want to spend a lot of time in the kitchen, especially in the summer when it's hot. Apricot jam is quick and easy; this recipe has only four ingredients. It will bring the flavor of summer to your toast, biscuits, pancakes, and waffles no matter what time of year. It also makes a delicious glaze for cake or a roasted chicken.

2 pounds very ripe apricots
¾ cup water
¼ cup lemon juice
1 cup raw Turbinado sugar

Wash the apricots well, then tear them in half and discard the pits.

Put them in a saucepan that has a wide bottom (for good stirring and even cooking). Add the water, lemon juice, and sugar to the pan, stirring and slowly bringing it to a low boil.

Reduce the heat to medium-low and continue cooking, stirring often. The apricot mixture will begin to get "mushy" and that is exactly what you want. This takes about 45 minutes.

To see if you have the right "jamminess," drop a spoonful of the mushy apricots onto a cold plate. Then, with your finger, draw a line in the dollop. If the apricots stay on either side of the line, it's ready to put into your sterilized jam jars. If not, continue to cook on low heat.

Chokecherry Jelly

MAKES ABOUT 8 PINT JARS

A jar of fresh chokecherry jelly was sent to us by our friend and cowgirl Sandi Miller LaDuke in North Dakota, made from the ripe, fresh-picked chokecherries that abound in and around her ranch.

Sandi says, "The Native Americans (Mandan, Arikara, and Hidatsa) who lived along the Missouri River in my neighborhood used chokecherries in dried pemican, used the juice as dye, and for medicinal purposes. I have read that chokecherry tea is helpful when experiencing stomach problems. (Side note . . . the pits contain cyanide!) I've used the chokecherries to make cordial, too. It's so smooth that it could be dangerous! Delightful!"

We are thrilled to share this with you.

3 ½–4 pounds chokecherries (will yield 3 ½ cups juice)
4 cups sugar
1 package (1.75-ounce) Sure-Jell pectin
1 tablespoon butter

Credit: Shutterstock

Rinse the chokecherries and remove any leaves or stems (whatever doesn't look like you'd want in your jelly!).

Put cleaned chokecherries into a large saucepan and add water to cover plus about 1 inch.

Cook them, stirring occasionally on medium heat or until the berries split and release the pits. Continue cooking and use a potato masher to squish out all the juice for an additional 10 minutes.

When you're down to skins and pits, dump the whole works into a cheesecloth-lined colander inside a huge bowl. Twist the cheesecloth to press out juice and let the cheesecloth drip overnight. If you prefer jam with bits of the pulp, leave the mixture the way it is!

(**Note:** If you're pressed for time, freeze the juice for later at this point.)

Measure the juice into a saucepan. Add the sugar to a separate bowl. Stir the pectin into the fruit juice. Add the butter and bring the juice mixture to a full rolling boil that won't stir down. At that point, quickly add the sugar, return to a boil, and boil for 1 minute, stirring constantly.

Remove from the heat source and skim off any foam.

Fill jars with the hot fruit mixture, leaving a bit of headspace. Wipe the top of the jars clean and seal.

Turn the jars upside down and put them in a large pot. Cover the jars with boiling water about 1 inch over the jars. Leave them until the water cools, then put them out on the counter to seal. You'll hear a "pop" to indicate the jars have sealed. Sometimes this process can take up to 24 hours! If it appears your jelly didn't set, give it some time to congeal. This may take up to 48 hours.

Cowgirls' Blackberry and Whiskey Jam

MAKES ABOUT 2 PINTS

The hardest part of this recipe is the picking. Yes, there are thorns to dodge, but to preserve the sweet, summery taste of blackberries is worth the effort. The little added kick of the whiskey (and we hope you use Pendleton—the cowgirls' choice!) just adds to the goodness.

2 pounds (4–5 cups) blackberries
2 cups sugar
¼ cup whiskey
2 tablespoons lemon juice
1 teaspoon vanilla extract

Wash and rinse the berries well and let them dry out a little.

Combine blackberries, sugar, whiskey, lemon juice, and vanilla in a large saucepan.

Bring the mixture to a low boil and cook, stirring frequently, for 20 minutes, until berries are tender. Mash the berries with a potato masher to help break them up.

Continue boiling, stirring constantly, until mixture has thickened and coats the back of a spoon, about 15 to 20 minutes.

Ladle the jam into sterilized jam jars or containers.

Store in your refrigerator until ready to eat.

Early Summer Strawberry Vinegar

MAKES ABOUT 2½ CUPS

When the season provides strawberries in abundance, it's time to use them in many ways—shortcakes, pies, jam, or eaten right off the vines in your garden. A flavored vinegar made with strawberries is a perfect way to extend early summer. This is a sweet and fruity vinegar that is great in salad dressings. Pour a little in a glass of sparkling water over ice for a wonderful summer refresher. And it makes a very pretty gift!

2 cups strawberries, washed and halved
2 cups white wine vinegar
½ cup sugar

Place cut strawberries in a medium-size, heatproof glass or ceramic bowl.

Bring the vinegar just to a boil. Let it cool and then pour it over the strawberries. Let strawberries and vinegar steep until they are cool.

Cover with plastic wrap and place in the refrigerator for 3 or 4 days. The vinegar should turn a lovely rose color.

Strain the vinegar into a stainless steel saucepan and discard the strawberries.

Bring the strawberry vinegar to a boil and add the ½ cup of sugar (or less if you want the vinegar less sweet) and let it boil for a few minutes. Let it cool on the stove, and when it's cool, store it in sterilized glass canning jars with lids or bottles with stoppers in the refrigerator.

This will keep for 3 months or more. (But we don't think it will last that long! It's that good.)

Elderberry Remedy Syrup

APPROXIMATELY 16 OUNCES (2 CUPS)

Jill was lucky enough to have an old and well-established elderberry tree in her backyard. She made good use of it, making wine and a medicinal syrup from the ripe berries. Elderberry syrup or extract has been shown to significantly improve or reduce cold and flu symptoms, and it may help you get over your symptoms faster, when taken at the first sign of illness. Jill would take 1 teaspoon when she felt like she needed an immune boost. And she cautions, DO NOT eat raw elderberries!

½ cup fresh, ripe elderberries, washed
   and stems removed
2 cups water
1 tablespoon minced fresh ginger
   (optional)
½–1 cup organic honey

Combine the elderberries, water, and ginger (if using) in a small saucepan over high heat and bring the mixture to a boil. Lower the heat and allow the mixture to simmer until the water has been reduced by half, about 20 minutes.

Transfer the cooked berries and liquid to a clean bowl and pour it through a fine mesh strainer to remove the berry skins. Use the back of a spoon to press on the berries in the strainer to extract all of the juice, then discard the small amount of pulp left in the strainer.

Allow the elderberry juice to cool to room temperature (so the heat doesn't harm the nutrients in the honey), then stir in the honey using a whisk to incorporate it smoothly. Then transfer the syrup into a sealed glass jar that you can store in your refrigerator. This syrup should keep well for at least 2 weeks when stored in the fridge, so if you don't think you'll use it all before then, feel free to freeze any extra. An ice cube tray is a great way to make single portions you can thaw into a juice glass.

Garlicky Dill Pickles

MAKES 4 QUART JARS

Who doesn't like a snappy pickle with their picnic sandwich, hamburger, or hot dog? We do! These pickles are also pretty darn good diced into your potato or egg salad. These last a long, long time in your icebox.

5 pounds pickling cucumbers
Fresh dill, stems removed so only the
    fluffy dill "leaves" remain and cut to
    the depth of your jar
8 large cloves garlic, peeled and
    halved
4 cups white vinegar, divided
6 cups water
½ cup canning or pickling salt

Clean and sterilize the canning jars and lids.

Gently wash any dirt and residue off of your cucumbers.

Fill a sink or a large bowl with cold water and place the cucumbers in the water, then add ¼ cup of white vinegar. Let the cucumbers stand in the water for 30 minutes while you prepare the other ingredients.

Wash your hands well and place two cloves of garlic and a sprig or two of dill in each clean jar. Use two cloves per jar for a strong garlic flavor.

Pierce each cucumber with a sharp knife before putting it into the jar. Tightly pack all your clean jars with the washed cucumbers.

In a large pot add the water, remaining vinegar, and pickling salt, and bring to a boil for 1 minute.

Using a glass measuring cup, scoop and pour the boiling brine into the stuffed jars leaving ¼ inch of headspace in each jar. Add the lid and ring to each jar, tightening evenly.

Carefully place the filled jars into a large, deep saucepan and add just enough hot water to cover the jars.

Place the lid on the pan and bring to a boil. Process for 10 minutes (start timing after the water has reached a boil).

Turn off the burner and use canning tongs to transfer the jars to a clean, thick towel on the counter. Let them stand for 24 hours to cool. The lids will make a "pop" noise as they cool. This is the jar sealing. Any jars that do not seal should be refrigerated.

Wait at least 3 weeks before opening so the flavors will develop— we think the waiting to enjoy is the hardest part.

EDIBLE FLOWERS AND
HOW TO USE THEM

Nature can provide you with more than just fruits and vegetables. If you plant any or all of these flowers, you have the added bonus of bright garnishes, good-for-you-in-every-way organic teas, and the bees will thank you many times over. Here are a few of our favorites that are easy to grow and look so pretty in the garden. Even a window box will do in a pinch!

Nasturtiums

These are our favorite because they add color and a peppery tang to a salad. They look wonderful on a cheese plate as decorations you can eat. Put one on a cracker and top with cheese.

Pansies

So pretty in a salad or on top of a homemade cupcake and so easy to grow!

Violets

You can use the leaves (washed, of course) in salads or cooked like spinach. Really! The flowers look so pretty on cupcakes and they make a wonderful jelly.

Credit: GettyImages/lacaosa

Grandma Mamie Mae Houston's Mesquite Bean Jelly

MAKES 8-10 HALF-PINT JARS

Mesquite is a common small tree native to the southwestern United States and Mexico. These trees have long been used by native people of the Southwest for food, medicine, beverages, firewood, construction material, and furniture making. We know it today for the distinctive flavor it adds to barbecue. The pods, sometimes called "beans," from these trees ripen from late June through September and are a golden-red color when ready to pick.

Rosa Lee's grandmother, Mamie Mae Houston, lived on the Sonoran Desert, near Tucson, Arizona. Grandma Mamie made this jelly every year, and Rosa Lee likely assisted her in gathering the mesquite tree pods. The sweet jelly turns a beautiful honey-brown color and is perfect for spreading over toast or biscuits. (That's Rosa Lee pictured here as a rootin' tootin' little cowgirl.)

1 gallon (16 cups) mesquite pods
1 package (1.75-ounce) Sure-Jell pectin
2 tablespoons lemon juice
7 cups sugar
Red food coloring (optional)

Wash the mesquite pods to remove bugs (!) and break the pods into pieces. Cover the pods with water, bring to a boil, and cook until they are tender.

Strain the cooked pods from the bean-infused juice while the liquid is still hot. Discard the cooked pods. This should yield about 4 ½ cups of juice.

Add the pectin to the hot liquid and bring to a full rolling boil.

Add the lemon juice and sugar. Cook this, stirring occasionally, for 5 minutes until thickened. The jelly will be a lovely golden color—almost like honey. (**Cowgirl tip:** Add a drop or two of red food coloring if you want it to look "fancy." This was Grandma Mamie's way of doing it.)

Spoon the jelly into clean and sterilized half-pint jars and seal.

Cowgirl tip: For mesquite syrup, omit the Sure-Jell and boil until the syrup falls off a spoon in a sheet. Perfect on pancakes, biscuits, and waffles. We would do french toast.

Credit: Courtesy of Lee Cooley

Lovely Lilac Jelly

MAKES 4 (8-OUNCE) JARS OR 8 (4-OUNCE) JARS

There are two things we like very, very much. One is cowgirls who saddle right up and gallop in to help no matter the situation, and the other is lilacs. The fragrance evokes our childhood somehow. We are willing to bet you did not know you can make a lovely jelly from lilac blossoms.

When we mentioned this to Katherine Whitney, she volunteered to make this for us, because, she said, "I have oodles of lilacs and my grandmother used to make jelly out of all sorts of things and I've never heard of lilac jelly." We gave her the go-ahead and she galloped out to her garden and back into her kitchen to produce small jars of a lovely honey-colored and faintly honey-tasting jelly. You can learn more about Katherine in the Sources at the end of the book. She is a talented jewelry maker and is our hero.

2 cups fresh lilac blossoms, free of any
    spray or pesticides, leaves and stems
    removed
2½ cups boiling water
¼ cup lemon juice
1 package (1.75-ounce) Sure-Jell pectin
4 cups sugar

First, brew a lilac tea by putting the blossoms into a heat resistant container (like stainless steel) and pouring boiling water over them. Let the blossoms steep for at least 8 hours.

Strain the blossoms out of the tea and discard them. You should have about 2¼ cups of lilac-infused water. Add a bit more water if needed.

Add the lilac tea, lemon juice, and pectin to a large pot and bring it to a rolling boil, stirring often.

Add the sugar and return to a boil. Boil this for 1 minute, stirring constantly.

Remove from the heat and skim off the foam.

Ladle the jelly into the sterilized jars, leaving about 1/4 inch of headspace. Wipe the rims clean and screw the lids on tight.

Process the jars in a deep, large pot of boiling water for 10 minutes.

Remove the jars and allow them to rest until they are cool. Wipe them dry and clean, check that the lids are on tight, and put on your labels (no one will believe you!).

BENEFITS OF LILAC

Lilac has been known to be a medicinal herb that can help lower fever and improve digestion. Its medicinal use has been documented since the Middle Ages.

You can make lilac tea using the blossoms (picked clean of stems and any debris). Wilt the blossoms and dry them completely. Then store them in an airtight jar.

To enjoy your cup of lilac tea, put about 2 tablespoons of the blossoms into an infuser. Pour boiling water into your cup with the infuser and let it steep about 3 to 4 minutes.

Honey sweetens this tea very nicely.

Robin's Remarkable Relish

MAKES ABOUT 2 CUPS

In the late summer, Robin gets a hankering to do a chutney, or a relish. She developed this relish to satisfy this urge and it is a favorite now—great on hamburgers, hot dogs, or meatloaf sandwiches. This is a small batch recipe so it doesn't require all that canning. But you could double or triple this recipe if you really wanted to have lots to share or keep over the long, cold winter.

2 pounds tomatoes, peeled and finely
   chopped
1 small sweet onion, finely chopped
2 sweet peppers (yellow or orange,
   but red would do, too), finely
   chopped
1 cup apple cider vinegar
½ cup packed brown sugar
½ teaspoon kosher salt (or canning salt)
½ teaspoon ground mustard
¾–1 teaspoon ground pumpkin pie
   spice

Add the ingredients to a medium saucepan. Stir to combine and bring the mixture to a boil over medium-high heat. Reduce the heat to a simmer, uncovered for 1 hour or more, until the relish has thickened.

When the relish is cool, place in a clean jar with a lid and keep in the fridge for a month.

If you increase this recipe, you can put the hot relish into pint jars, leaving ½ inch of headspace. Process the jars in a boiling water bath for 20 minutes.

Rosemary for Remembrance Oil

MAKES ABOUT 2 CUPS

We always have a bottle of rosemary oil in our kitchen. It is our go-to ingredient when we roast a chicken or a of pan root vegetables. Try it on pasta or over fresh tomatoes. Rosemary oil makes a beautiful gift with its deep green color and it smells like heaven.

3 or 4 sprigs (1 cup) fresh rosemary
2 cups olive oil

Wash the fresh rosemary under cold, running water, then dry thoroughly. Strip the leaves from the stems, crushing them between your palms to begin releasing their fragrant oils.

Put the olive oil in a small saucepan (not aluminum).

Add the rosemary leaves to the saucepan and place the pan over low heat on your stove. Heat the rosemary oil for 5 to 10 minutes, stirring constantly. As the oil warms up, it will begin to smell like rosemary, but if the oil begins bubbling, it is too hot.

Reduce the heat, stir, and let this sit until completely cool.

Place a metal colander in a large metal bowl. Pour the oil mixture into the colander to strain out the rosemary leaves. Discard the leaves.

Once the oil has cooled to room temperature, it can be poured into a clean bottle and capped or corked. Label the bottle with the bottling date and the ingredients used. Do not add any rosemary to the bottle. It looks pretty, but it can cause harmful bacteria to grow in the oil. This will keep for up to 2 months at room temperature if you keep it away from direct light, or 6 months in your refrigerator.

Sweet Cheeks Salsa

MAKES 2 CUPS

If your garden has surprised you with an abundance of tomatoes, or you stop at a farmers' market and see bushels of red and ripe tomatoes, we urge you to make this salsa. Unlike "fresh" salsa made with fresh tomatoes, onion, and peppers, this salsa is slowly simmered to thick perfection. We like its "sweet" notes instead of the (sometimes) surprise of salsa gone too hot! This salsa freezes well. It's the perfect salsa to enjoy with the chips of your choice while the steaks are grilling. We scrambled two farm fresh eggs, put some of this salsa on top, a dollop of sour cream, and a few slices of ripe avocado, and it was the Best Lunch Ever.

8 large, ripe tomatoes, peeled* and chopped
1 sweet onion, peeled and chopped
1 (4-ounce) can green chilies, seeded and chopped
1 (8-ounce) can sliced black olives, drained
3 tablespoons packed brown sugar
1 clove garlic, peeled and smashed
1 teaspoon dried oregano
½ teaspoon ground cumin
Salt and pepper, to taste

In a large saucepan, combine all the ingredients and bring to a low boil over medium heat.

Simmer this mixture, stirring now and then, until the salsa has reached a thick consistency, about 2 to 3 hours.

Taste and adjust the seasonings before ladling the salsa into sterilized glass jars (makes a great gift) or you can store this in the refrigerator.

*Cowgirl tip: Want to learn how to quickly peel tomatoes? Fill the pot you are going to use for the salsa with water and bring it to a boil. Drop in the tomatoes, one by one, for about 2 to 3 minutes. Using a slotted spoon, remove them to a drain board and let them cool. The skin will drop right off! Empty the water, wash the pan, and proceed with the rest of the recipe.

Credit: Marion Adams

Traffic Jam

MAKES 6 CUPS

Maude Banning, a cowgirl we know who is clever with anything edible, sent us this rather odd (at first) jam recipe. She said, "When I make this and put it in the pantry, the hired hands make so many trips to it with a spoon I just call it 'Traffic Jam.'" Since both of us always buy too many bananas, and we are tired of banana bread, this recipe is perfect and easy to make. And, yes, we make several trips to the opened jar, too. And PS? It's great on banana bread.

12 ripe bananas, peeled and diced
6 oranges, peeled and diced (no pith)
4 lemons, peeled and sliced (no pith)
1½ cups sugar

Add the fruit to a large bowl and mix. Put 2 cups of fruit into a saucepan and add the sugar (for every 2 cups of fruit, add 1½ cups of sugar).

Stir over low heat until the sugar dissolves, then bring this to a boil and boil rapidly for 20 minutes until jam coats the back of a spoon.

Put the cooled jam into your canning jars and screw the lids on tight!

FOOD SAFETY AND SANITATION TIPS FOR THE GREAT OUTDOORS

It isn't fun getting sick in the great outdoors from eating bad food, and it will definitely ruin your trip. In general, you can pack-in food that needs to be kept cool or hot usually for a three-day window providing you are using coolers and have ways to heat up your food. Longer than that, you should consider foods that don't need to be kept hot or cold, including shelf-stable things like fresh fruit, canned goods, dry grains, bread, and nuts. You can also purchase instant/dehydrated/freeze-dried products available at outdoor stores that only need hydration and a little heat to serve.

If you are traveling in an RV with the capacity to refrigerate food, you only need to make sure that the refrigerator is keeping the proper temperature while you are on the road. However, many RVs do not have the capacity to run a refrigerator while traveling. In this case, you will also need to use coolers, but then you can switch over to the refrigerator once you reach your destination.

Our good friend and Chef Instructor Clive Wanstall, CCE, who teaches at Lane Community College here in Oregon graciously contributed his words of culinary wisdom regarding food safety in the wild.

Wanstall says, "I like to pre-prepare as much food as possible and just toss together and/or finish cook with little fussing."

He also recommends his Bare Bones Basics for campers to remember, which are:

1. Keep it cold or keep it hot.

2. Keep preparation on-site to a minimum.

3. Cook and eat promptly.

4. Avoid leftovers (make enough, but not too much).

The first concept is keeping your food either cold or hot. Food needs to be kept out of what's called the "danger zone"—temperatures between 40 to 140°F—for more than two to four hours. These in-the-middle temperatures are when bacteria can grow easily and make your sick. Cooking out of doors or taking food to eat outdoors needs more thought to help keep food safe on the trip. Here are some tips:

- Pre-chill all your food before you put it in the cooler.

- Start with frozen food—it will defrost and it will help keep things cool in the cooler.

- Have two coolers—one for drinks and one for food.

- Use blue ice or freeze your fresh water or juice in bottles or milk cartons, as well as ice.

- Pack your cooler tight, with fewer air gaps (think 60 percent food and 40 percent ice).

- Layer your food and ice—a layer of ice on the bottom and then meats, more ice, and other food, with ice on the top to finish off with your more delicate items.

- Keep your cooler in the shade or cover it with a towel or blanket.

- Think about keeping a refrigerator thermometer in your coolers.

- Take extra caution with raw meat, making sure it is located in the coldest places in the cooler.

- Invest in an insta-read thermometer and make sure that you are cooking meat to the highest minimum temperature. According to Chef Wanstall, the most recent temperature guidelines are as follows:

  - Chicken and reheated foods: 165°F

  - Ground beef, pork, and lamb: 155°F

  - Fish and steak/chops (beef, pork, and lamb): 145°F

Keeping it all clean is also very important to protect the food you serve from any contamination. Be very careful, as an example, not to work with meats and then start working with prepping vegetables on the same cutting board without sanitizing and also washing your hands.

Being organized also helps food safety and makes for a much more relaxing time cooking outdoors. The more prep work you can accomplish at home before you go, the better. Look at the things you want to serve and think about what might be done ahead of time. If a recipe calls for diced onions, dice them at home and then put them in a plastic bag. This goes for measuring out ingredients and even starting a recipe that can be finalized on your trip. Take pre-measured and prepped ingredients whenever possible. Chef Wanstall also suggests freezer-quality zip-top bags.

Here are some more tips for organizing your cooking station:

- Wash your hands frequently when preparing food. Designate a hand wash area (away from food preparation if you can). No water for hand washing? Take sanitizing wipes and use them often.

- Use latex gloves for food preparation on the trip.

- Clean your cooking area before and after your cooking project.

- Prep raw meats away from other food products you are preparing, including using a separate cutting board for meat.

- Take Band-Aids along in case of knife cuts.

- Wrap your cooking utensils in plastic for transport.

- Put your food in containers or plastic, so it doesn't get soaked with melting ice.

- Take the smallest amounts of ingredients, just the amounts you need to use.

SOURCES

Cast Iron

Look up Lodge Manufacturing Company at lodgemfg.com for any questions you might have. This is a good company! They can help.

Cowgirl Books

In addition to being a great cowgirl, Janice Gilbertson has been writing and sharing cowboy and western poetry for more than twenty years. Her poetry book's title poem, "Sometimes, in the Lucias" won WWA's Spur Finalist award in 2009 and her debut novel, *Summer of '58*, was published by Pen-L Publishing in 2015. Her follow-up novel, *The Canyon House*, was a Women Writing the West's 2017 WILLA Literary Award finalist. Her work has also appeared in *She Speaks to Me: Western Women's View of the West through Poetry and Song*, compiled by Jill Charlotte Stanford (TwoDot, 2016). In 2020, she published her first horror novel, *The Dark Side of Gibson Road*.

Janice was born and raised in Pine Canyon, west of King City, California, in an area known for being part of "John Steinbeck Country." This is where she still lives, writes, and rides today.

Want to read more about packing and cooking in the wilderness?

A Cowgirl's Life in the Woods by Lauralee Northcott will have you yearning for a good horse, a pack saddle, a camping spot, and Lauralee as your companion. Her poetry is wonderful, she knows her way around cast iron camp cooking, and she can sing too! You can find her book on her website, lauraleenoethcott.com, Barnes and Noble, or Amazon. Happy Trails!

Cowgirl Gifts

We'd like to introduce you to Gina Keesling, creator of hoofprints.com, where you will find unique items she has gathered that are suitable for gifts for you, your horse, and your farrier. She describes her life as, "Fun on the farm; running a business from home, fixing the home, nurturing high maintenance animals & trying to stay sane!"

Check out her unique products for the equine professional at hoofprints.com or read about her adventures on her blog, ginakeesling.wordpress.com/. You can follow Gina on social media, too (facebook.com/farriers.hoofprints).

Omnia Oven

Now about that "oven" that Robin and Jim take on all their adventures in a small RV that has no oven, just a propane stovetop. This is what they use and swear by!

With the Omnia recreational oven you can serve freshly baked breads and tasty casseroles cooked on your stovetop. Almost everything that can be heated, baked, or cooked in a fixed, domestic oven can be baked in an Omnia on the hot plate. Think oven, think Omnia! Visit omniasweden.com/en/home/.

Katherine Whitney

INDEX

MEET THE COWGIRL COOKS

Jill Charlotte Stanford is the author of *The Cowgirl's Cookbook: Recipes for Your Home on the Range*; *You Might Be a Cowgirl If . . .: A Guide to Life on the Range*; *Keep Cookin' Cowgirl: More Recipes for Your Home on the Range*; *Cowgirls in the Kitchen: Recipes, Tales, and Tips for a Home on the Range* (with coauthor Robin Betty Johnson); and *She Speaks to Me: Western Women's View of the West through Poetry and Song*. Jill lives and writes in Sisters, Oregon. Researching and speaking to groups about the old-time cowgirls are what she loves best, along with cooking and eating, of course.

Robin Betty Johnson was given a toy stove powered by a light bulb when she was little and has not looked back. She attended Lane Community College's culinary arts program and then became an instructor in the program. Robin now lives and cooks in Portland, Oregon, with her husband, Jim, who has enjoyed a good many of the recipes in this book and who built most of the campfires.